The Data-Driven Leader

Leveraging Data and AI to Create Business Impact

Sandro Saitta

Technics Publications
SEDONA, ARIZONA

TECHNICS PUBLICATIONS

115 Linda Vista, Sedona, AZ 86336 USA
https://www.TechnicsPub.com

Edited by Steve Hoberman
Cover design by Lorena Molinari

First Printing 2025

Copyright © 2025 by Sandro Saitta

ISBN, print ed.   9798898160289
ISBN, Kindle ed.   9798898160296
ISBN, PDF ed.   9798898160302

To my parents, for teaching me perseverance.

To my wife Rana, for her unwavering support.

To my kids, for keeping me young.

Endorsements

There are many things to like about this clear and concise book, but my favorite aspect of it is that it describes all forms of AI and puts generative AI in perspective. If you want to understand the role of data, analytics, and AI in your organization, this is a great place to start.

**Thomas H. Davenport, Distinguished Professor, Babson College
Research Fellow, MIT Initiative on the Digital Economy
Author of "Competing on Analytics", "All In on AI", and "All Hands on Tech"**

AI without data is like a rocket without fuel. In "The Data-Driven Leader", Sandro Saitta begins exactly where every book on AI should—with data—then takes you on a practical, well-illustrated, business-savvy journey into the future.

**Douglas B. Laney, data, analytics, and AI strategy advisor
Author of "Infonomics" and "Data Juice"**

Right up front, "No data, no AI." Way to focus attention where it belongs, Sandro!

Tom Redman, "The Data Doc", Advisor, Author, "People and Data"

Every AI system hinges on data. Yet data is always slanted by the humans who collected it -- the notion of 'raw' data is only a myth, as author Sandro Saitta prudently points out. In "The Data-Driven Leader", he delivers a refreshingly friendly and clear overview of the data fundamentals that every professional needs to know. If you're a business professional—or even a data scientist in training—and you'd like to dig into the nuts-and-bolts practices that bolster data's fundamental integrity and value, then look no further."

**Eric Siegel, Ph.D., CEO of Gooder AI
Author of "The AI Playbook" and "Predictive Analytics"**

"The Data-Driven Leader" tackles what I genuinely thought was impossible: making data and AI approachable for literally every professional out there. This book doesn't just succeed at that impossible task—it has this wonderful side effect of making our entire field more inclusive and welcoming.

The biggest hurdle for getting more people to work in and with data and AI has always been rooted in intimidation. The technology feels overwhelming, the jargon is impenetrable, and confidence (or lack thereof)? That's usually the silent killer of all initial motivation. But this book—especially written in Sandro's refreshingly clear style—doesn't just give you knowledge. It builds up that confidence along the way. What really got me were the examples throughout the book that make everything tangible and, more importantly, actionable.

If you've been looking for that one place to finally get started with data & AI, this is it. No prerequisites, no intimidation factor, just solid learning that meets you exactly where you are. A must-read for anyone curious about this field - because that should be everyone at this point.

Tiankai Feng
Author of "Humanizing Data Strategy" and "Humanizing AI Strategy"

At a prior company, I had the pleasure of working with Sandro as we built many of the fundamental AI services from the ground up. There, I witnessed his talent for turning complexity into significant business value through data. In this book, he brings that same clarity and expertise to every page—an indispensable resource for anyone seeking to leverage data and AI in real-world applications.

Dan Hill, Head of Machine Learning and AI, On

This book is a must-read for executives aiming to understand AI in a business context. Authored by a seasoned practitioner, it delivers a clear and practical overview of the technology, enriched with real-world examples. It strikes the perfect balance—accessible without being simplistic, and informative without being overly technical. A compelling introduction to AI implementation that speaks directly to the challenges and opportunities leaders face today.

René Monnard, Innovation and Technology Lead
Global Product Protection, Takeda Pharmaceuticals

Clear, concise, and deeply grounded in core business and statistical principles, this book delivers exactly what Sandro Saitta promises. With rich examples drawn from his diverse experience, it offers a practical and insightful look under the hood of Machine Learning and Artificial Intelligence. If you believe your business data holds the key to smarter decision-making, this is the book for you. It's not just theory—it's actionable, with a curated list of further readings for those who want to explore more. But be warned: success depends on the quality of your business questions and your data. Without these, even the most advanced AI tools fall short. A must-read. Five stars!

Marcel Baumgartner, former Data Analytics Expert at Nestlé

I thoroughly enjoyed reading this book from beginning to end. It progressively and pedagogically presents all the problems that data professionals encounter every day (data quality, dashboarding, AI, Gen AI etc.). Although we are immersed in the world of data every day, it is often difficult to take a step back to popularize a concept that seems obvious to us to non-initiated people. Sandro deserves a great deal of credit in each chapter of this book because he effectively and skillfully popularizes concepts and makes them easy to understand. I recommend this book to anyone who would like to get started in the world of data, and I will personally promote it within my professional circle.

Hatem Hamza, Head of Data, Hublot

This book is a great companion for business managers on their journey to better understand the power and challenges of AI in its many facets. The book sheds light on many relevant topics such as the importance of data, AI, generative AI, and machine learning. With the right balance between theory and practical examples, it explains these things at a level of granularity accessible to everyone.

Dr. Frank Block
Product Manager Advanced Analytics & AI, Platforms and Frameworks, Roche

A good read to introduce Data and AI literacy elements, to the point. A companion for training workshops written by an expert trainer, and not forgetting the Data in AI.

Eloy Sasot, Chief Data Officer, ASML

"The Data-Driven Leader" addresses a critical business topic, detailing both the opportunities and challenges. Backed by real-world experience, it offers practical insights for navigating today's data-driven landscape.

Dr. Erik Beulen
Independent member of the Data Committee of Royal FloraHolland
Professor of Information Management at the University of Manchester

Sandro Saitta's book is an essential read for anyone navigating a data-driven environment. As a practitioner, I truly appreciate the seamless blend of theoretical concepts and practical insights. What stands out most to me is the hands-on advice, such as 'fail fast' and embracing failure as part of the learning process—especially relevant in the ever-evolving age of AI.

Dr. Sina Wulfmeyer, Chief Data Officer, Unique AI

Data is the new gold, and AI is on the hype, but many leaders still overlook how deeply interconnected these two domains truly are. Sandro bridges this gap with clarity and precision, offering a comprehensive perspective on the critical role of Data Culture/Mindset in modern organizations. Through practical examples and strategic insights, he equips readers with the tools to navigate and embrace the disruptive potential of new technologies. A must have read!

Jérôme MICHAUD, Innovation Manager, Geneva Airport

Contents

Foreword

In today's world, where generative AI dominates the headlines, it is easy for business leaders to get caught up in the hype. When I first started working with data and AI, I quickly realized how overwhelming the topic can feel, especially if you do not come from a technical background. Like many leaders, I was looking, both for myself and for other decision makers, for clear, simple guidance.

From my own experience leading digital and data upskilling initiatives, I have learned how essential it is to bring leaders on board and provide them with the right skills. Without a solid understanding of data and AI basics, it is difficult to make responsible decisions or drive real innovation. That is how we launched our first classroom training sessions for leaders, together with Sandro. His ability to break down complex topics was truly impressive and made the learning experience engaging, approachable, and highly relevant, even for people without a technical background.

Over the past few years, I have had the chance to work closely with Sandro on both virtual and classroom training. What I have always appreciated most is the way he can take advanced concepts and make them simple, understandable, and meaningful for decision makers. You do not need to be a data scientist to follow along—and that is exactly why his approach works so well.

Having all this knowledge summarized in a book is a tremendous added value. *The Data-Driven Leader* gives leaders and decision makers across all functions—whether in HR, Marketing, Finance, or any other domain—an easy way to discover the concepts, apply them in their own work, and build the confidence to ask the right questions. It is the perfect starting point for anyone who wants to navigate the world of data and AI with clarity, confidence, and responsibility.

Nicole Pfister, Global Solutions Learning Manager, Global Marketing & Customer Insights, Roche Diagnostics

Acknowledgments

Thanks to everyone who supported me, in one way or another, through discussions, ideas, and motivation to write this book. I am particularly grateful to those who endorsed and provided feedback on the book. It greatly improved the quality of the manuscript: Tom Redman, Eric Siegel, Tom Davenport, Doug Laney, Tiankai Feng, Dean Abbott, Nicole Pfister, Eloy Sasot, Dan Hill, Frank Block, Hatem Hamza, Marcel Baumgartner, Jérôme Koller, René Monnard, Carsten Dehner, Sina Wulfmeyer, Jérôme Michaud, and Erik Beulen.

A big thank you to Steve Hoberman and the Technics Publications team for their trust and support during the revision process. It was a pleasure working with you. Finally, I would like to thank my wife and kids for their patience, especially during the final stages of the writing process.

Introduction

In today's dynamic business landscape, where the widespread concepts of digital transformation and predictive technologies dominate discussions, many companies, including Sarah's, increasingly recognize the profound potential of data and Artificial Intelligence (AI). They witnessed AI becoming ubiquitous, from enhancing cross-selling to optimizing existing processes, and observed competitors gaining a tangible edge through data-driven decisions. Yet, this burgeoning awareness was often accompanied by a significant challenge: a lack of clarity on how to proceed. The sheer volume of technical terminology, the rapidly evolving trends, and the absence of a clear, actionable roadmap left many decision makers feeling overwhelmed and uncertain about initiating their own data and AI projects.

Sarah, a seasoned executive within this environment, was no stranger to this constant buzz, much of it seeming like distant, technical jargon. While her company had long relied on established reports and managerial intuition, the growing precision and speed of data-informed decisions from rivals became impossible to ignore. A particularly challenging sales forecasting meeting, where traditional expert knowledge proved insufficient, served as a turning point. It wasn't just about adopting a new technology, she realized, but about addressing a fundamental gap in understanding. For her organization to truly leverage this power, the path forward lay in demystification and widespread literacy concerning data and AI, rather than blindly chasing the latest algorithmic trends.

Her journey, and the core philosophy of "The Data-Driven Leader", began with a foundational truth: "No data, no AI". Sarah understood that to effectively lead initiatives, make informed decisions, and engage meaningfully with data specialists, she needed to grasp the essential role of data as a sustainable, endless energy source for any AI endeavor. This book, much like Sarah's crucial realization, is crafted for decision makers. It offers a business-focused introduction, replete with concrete use cases and practical insights, designed to empower leaders to effectively communicate with data specialists and strategically apply AI within their organizations.

Why I wrote this book

I have been working in the field of data and AI for the past 20 years. I have also been teaching data and AI-related topics for the past 10 years. I have prepared talks, courses, and exercises to deliver to hundreds of people, most of them at the manager and executive level. As explained in the foreword, I have met countless leaders with a wish to understand the field of data and AI better. I have worked on data and AI projects for or with companies in various industries, including telco, chemicals, consumer goods, online travel agencies, banking, insurance, pharma, recruitment, perfume, food processing, computer hardware, energy, and many others. Thanks to this experience, I have compiled content about data and AI, which I think will be useful to every decision maker and any leader.

There are many books about AI out there. Most of them fall into one of these categories: on one side of the spectrum, the books on coding and algorithms. On the other side, there are books with a high-level view of AI, for example, within digital transformation. I think there are not enough books that i) have a business-focused view, ii) cover both data and AI, and iii) contain concrete use cases and related tips and tricks from the trenches.

Why you need this book

This book is aimed at decision makers and business leaders with an interest in knowing more about data and AI. For a decision maker, this means being able to understand and communicate data effectively. This also implies AI literacy, encompassing an understanding of machine learning, data science, and generative AI. As written in "Data is Everybody's Business":

Data is not just for people with 'data' in their job title.

The theme of "The Data-Driven Leader" is business focus, as well as several use cases illustrating the different concepts. There is no equation, no detailed algorithm, no pseudo-code, and no programming languages—simply concepts and examples. Note that this book can also be used as a companion material for the various training and workshops I provide through my company, viadata (www.viadata.ch).

You have to learn about data and AI nowadays. AI is omnipresent, as explained in "Prediction Machines":

> *AI is everywhere – packing into your phone's apps, optimizing your electricity grids, and replacing your stock portfolio managers.*

In "The Data-Driven Leader", you will travel from the starting point (data), through AI and Generative AI, to conclude with the limits of such approaches. Having a big picture about both data and AI topics will help you navigate the data-driven transformation with higher self-confidence.

My objective is to provide a short business-oriented introduction to both data and AI. Concepts are reinforced through examples and illustrations. We focus both on data and AI (and not only AI). First, because any AI is based on data, it is essential to have basic notions about data. And second, you can generate insights from data using statistics and visualization, among others. AI is definitely not necessary in all situations. Hopefully, after reading this book, you will know how AI works and when to use it (or not).

Structure

The book is structured to follow a flow from data itself to statistics, visualization, and AI. It continues with AI applications, Generative AI, best practices, and concludes with limits and trends in AI. Here is the detailed structure of the book:

- **It all starts with data**: Explains the foundational role of data in any AI project. It illustrates why data is never neutral and how data collection methods impact the outcomes of AI initiatives.

- **You need quality data**: Highlights the importance of clean, complete, and consistent data to ensure model reliability. It presents practical ways to assess and improve data quality before using the data.

- **Summary statistics wanted**: Introduces basic statistical concepts that help understand and explore data. It covers measures like mean, median, and correlation to identify trends[1] and potential insights early.

- **The art of data visualization:** Demonstrates how charts and plots can turn complex data into clear insights. It

---

[1] In this book we use the term "trend" and "pattern" to refer to the signal available in the data.

focuses on tailoring visuals to different audiences and telling compelling data stories.

- **Machines that learn**: Provides a simple explanation of how machine learning works. It describes the key types of models and how they are trained to make predictions or find trends.

- **AI in practice**: Presents real-world use cases where AI adds value, from sales forecasting to behavioral targeting. It emphasizes that AI is a tool to solve business problems—not a goal in itself.

- **Generative AI and chatbots**: Explains tools that create new content, such as text or images. It explains how these models work, how to use them effectively, and what challenges they introduce.

- **Best practices in data science**: Outlines the steps to start and manage a data project successfully. It provides guidance on idea generation, use case selection, and project prioritization.

- **Limits and trends in AI**: Addresses the current constraints of AI, including overfitting, bias, and lack of explainability. It also looks at future directions, such as trustworthy AI and regulations.

- **Conclusion**: Wraps up the book by encouraging continued learning and responsible use of data. It reinforces the message that becoming data-driven is a journey, not a one-time effort.

This book can be seen as a starting point for learning more about data and AI. This is why I provide several references to valuable books in the field. I reference the books either in the text or at the end of each chapter.

More information

Such boxes appear throughout the book. They contain further details about the topic, specific examples, or personal experiences I would like to share with you. While you can skip them and still understand all the concepts in the book, they provide the personal touch and my view on the fields of Data and AI.

All the terms used in this book will be explained in the text. You can find a glossary at the very end of the book. The central assumption made during writing is to use the term AI in a broad sense. Once further terms are explained, I will switch to these concepts, such as machine learning and data science, for example.

ONE

Everything Starts with Data

AI relies entirely on data. Without data, there is no AI. But data is not neutral. It is the result of decisions about what to measure, how to collect it, and what to leave out. This chapter explains why data is never raw and why understanding its origin is essential. It presents different types of data and the primary methods used to collect them. It also shows how bias appears early in the process and how it affects the quality of AI models. Through examples, the chapter helps to see why careful choices are needed before any AI project begins.

No data, no AI

Without data, there is no AI. Data is at the heart of every AI initiative. As noted in "Data-Driven Business Transformation":

> *Data is so much more than the new oil,*
> *it is the sustainable endless energy source*
> *we have been looking for.*

In this book, we define data as facts, measurements, or observations collected from various sources. Contrary to popular belief, data is never *raw*. Indeed, we speak of raw data as independent from human bias. If we take poll data as an example: specific questions are asked to a subset of the population. Therefore, the available data, even when not processed, is biased.

Every dataset is shaped by human decisions: what to measure, how to collect it, and what to exclude. The process of gathering data is fundamental, as it defines the quality, reliability, and ultimately, the success of data-driven insights.

Data is not new, but the way people and companies deal with it is evolving. As stated in "The Digital Transformation Playbook" by David Rogers:

> *Many companies that have used data as a specific part of*
> *their operations for years are now discovering a data*
> *revolution: data is coming from new sources, being*
> *applied to new problems, and becoming a key driver of*
> *innovation.*

Since data is at the heart of dashboards, analytics, and AI, decision makers need to understand related concepts and envision its importance for the company.

> ### Singular or plural?
>
> Data is technically the plural of datum. As the quantity of data is often important, we could be tempted to use it in a plural form. However, it is also well accepted in the singular form. In this book, we will use the singular form.

Leveraging data with AI

For a company, expanding revenue streams often means looking inward, identifying opportunities to offer existing customers products they do not yet have. Traditionally, this might involve broad, generalized campaigns, but leveraging data and AI provides a far more precise approach: cross-selling. By analyzing comprehensive customer data, encompassing transaction history, service usage, demographics, and past interactions, the company could build sophisticated profiles. AI models then predict which additional products or services a customer is most likely to be interested in, long before they might even consider it themselves.

The impact of such an initiative can be transformative. Imagine marketing efforts shifting from generic mass outreach to personalized recommendations, leading to a significant increase in conversion rates and overall customer value. This data-driven strategy not only boosts revenue but also enhances customer satisfaction by presenting relevant offers at opportune moments, fostering deeper loyalty.

However, the journey to effective cross-selling with AI is not without its hurdles. Key challenges often revolve around ensuring the quality and completeness of customer data, as incomplete or inaccurate records can lead to flawed predictions and missed opportunities. Additionally, building customer trust and navigating ethical considerations surrounding data privacy and personalized targeting are paramount. Over-relying on predictions without human oversight can also lead to missteps, highlighting the need for a balanced approach.

The foundational concepts of data, the specifics of how machines learn, and the practical implementation of AI applications (including their limits and challenges), are precisely what "The Data-Driven Leader" aims to demystify, providing a comprehensive guide for decision makers.

Different kinds of data

In "Data & AI Literacy", Bill Schmarzo defines data as:

> *[...] individual facts, statistics, or pieces of information that are collected through observation or measurement.*

Data can be classified as structured or unstructured. Structured data includes numeric and categorical variables. Unstructured data includes text, images, and videos, among others. As written in "Telling Your Data Story", Scott Taylor recommends starting with structured data:

> *Unstructured data offers loads of analytical promise, insight, and value, but you need structured data first for your organization.*

Let's start with typical numeric and categorical data. Here is an example of the different types of data you will encounter in your datasets (see Figure 1).

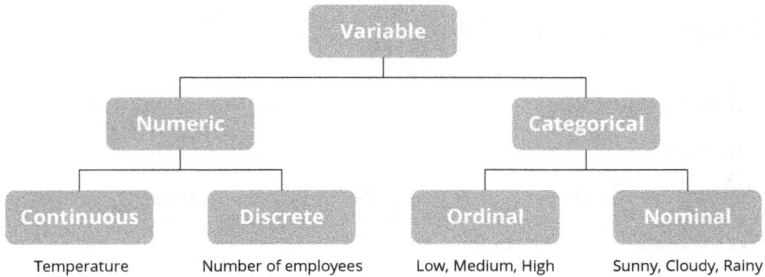

Figure 1: The different types of variables in structured data (with examples).

What is so special about data? Well, the huge advantage of data, including all datasets, is that it is reusable. As explained in "The Economics of Data, Analytics and Digital Transformation," Bill Schmarzo says:

> *The ability to reuse the same data sets across multiple use cases at near-zero marginal cost is the real economic game-changer.*

Data and analytics, if you leverage them properly, give your company a competitive advantage. With your company data, you can therefore compete with analytics. As explained in "Competing on Analytics":

> We define an analytical competitor as an organization that uses analytics extensively and systematically to outthink and outexecute the competition.

The myth of raw data

An expression like "*the data doesn't lie*" is often heard in business and technology discussions. Yet, this statement overlooks a crucial reality: data is never neutral. As Nick Barrowman aptly states in "Why Data is Never Raw":

> How data is constructed, recorded, and collected is the result of human decisions.

Keep in mind that data can also be incorrect or fail to tell the whole story.

Consider polling data, where survey results may exclude homeless individuals or people without internet access. Similarly, domestic violence statistics can be underestimated because many cases go unreported. These examples illustrate that data collection is an active process shaped by choices, constraints, and, at times, unintended biases.

Look beyond available data

Readily available data may not be enough to solve the use case you have in mind. The main reason is that data from existing systems (think a machine in a factory, for example) has been collected for testing and debugging purposes, not for AI. So "big data" does not mean "right data". Still, you need to start somewhere. So, if part of the required data is there, start with what you have. Then, collect additional data while you work on the present use case.

Methods of data collection

Organizations have several approaches to collecting data, each with its own advantages and challenges. We listed these approaches to open your mind to the different ways you can gather data for your company. These include:

- **Measuring**: Businesses use sensors, trackers, and devices to collect direct observations. For example, a security solution company employs track-and-trace solutions that utilize handheld devices to analyze spectral signals and verify product authenticity. This generates data for each measurement.

- **Purchasing**: Companies like Consumer Packaged Goods (CPGs) buy consumer data to refine their marketing strategies. Additionally, aggregated market data can be purchased to gain a better understanding of competitors.

- **Scraping**: Online companies, such as online travel agencies (OTA), extract data from websites to enhance their service offerings. Note that data quality is a big challenge regarding scraped data.

- **Crowdsourcing**: Some organizations rely on user-generated content or community-based reporting to gather valuable information. For example, an OTA can use such an approach to validate results from a deduplication algorithm.

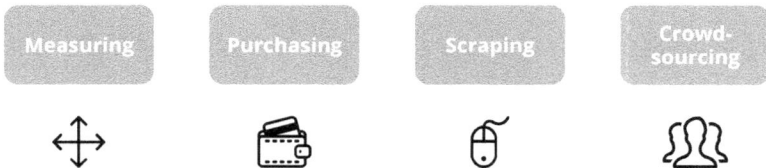

Figure 2: Illustration of four different ways to collect data in a company.

In addition, you can leverage existing data within your company. Common sources of information include Enterprise Resource Planning (ERP) and Customer Relationship Management (CRM) systems.

Collecting data with a captcha

In the last few years, a new and clever way to collect data has emerged. CAPTCHA is a way to detect humans from bots on a website, for example. It can ask the user to write the two words in the image. The tools already know the correct spelling of one of the two words (let's say the first one). If the user enters the first one correctly, it considers the second word entered as the correct spelling for the text on the image. While the tool verifies you are a human, it also collects new data to improve its computer vision algorithms.

A typical data set

Examining a concrete dataset will help clarify the various concepts we will discuss in this book. The dataset below is well-suited to introduce and explain machine learning in general.

To illustrate explicitly what we mean by data, let's discuss a concrete example with the Iris dataset. The Iris dataset consists of 150 samples of flowers from three different categories (setosa, virginica, and versicolor). Four features are measured on each flower: sepal length, sepal width, petal length, and petal width. Figure 3 shows a representation of a sample of the Iris dataset into rows and columns. We present it in this manner, as it is the most common way to display data in AI projects. Each row is a different sample (flower in this case), and each column is one of the features (information measured on the flower).

Columns (features)

	Sepal length	Sepal width	Petal length	Petal width	Class
	5.1	3.5	1.4	0.2	Iris-setosa
	4.9	3.0	1.4	0.2	Iris-setosa
	4.7	3.2	1.3	0.2	Iris-setosa
	4.6	3.1	1.5	0.2	Iris-setosa
	5.0	3.6	1.4	0.2	Iris-setosa
	5.4	3.9	1.7	0.4	Iris-setosa
Rows	4.6	3.4	1.4	0.3	Iris-setosa
(samples)	5.0	3.4	1.5	0.2	Iris-setosa
	4.4	2.9	1.4	0.2	Iris-setosa
	4.9	3.1	1.5	0.1	Iris-setosa
	5.4	3.7	1.5	0.2	Iris-setosa
	4.8	3.4	1.6	0.2	Iris-setosa
	4.8	3.0	1.4	0.1	Iris-setosa
	4.3	3.0	1.1	0.1	Iris-setosa
	5.8	4.0	1.2	0.2	Iris-setosa
	5.7	4.4	1.5	0.4	Iris-setosa

Figure 3: Example of the Iris dataset with rows (samples) and columns (features). (Source: Fisher, R. (1936). Iris [Dataset]. UCI Machine Learning Repository. https://doi.org/10.24432/C56C76).

Let's take another example with customer data: each row could be a customer, and each column could be any information you have about your customer (age, gender, address, preferences, etc.). One significant part of any data or AI project is to build such a dataset. We will share more information about the data science process in Chapter 8.

While this is an example of structured data, as mentioned earlier, data can also be unstructured. This includes text, images, videos, and more. Unstructured data usually lies in a special kind of database that handles this kind of data efficiently (often in cloud environments). Leveraging unstructured data is discussed further in the section on Generative AI and chatbots (see Chapter 7).

When exploring a dataset to understand it better, we often use the term metadata. Metadata is simply data about data. Basic information about a dataset could include the number of rows (samples), the number of columns (features), the type of each column (number, string, date, etc.), minimum and maximum values for numeric variables, etc. Metadata is key, as it is usually the visible part of data for decision makers.

Understanding and mitigating data bias

Since you make decisions based on data, realize that bias is present in every dataset. Bias is an inherent challenge in data collection. Since most data is generated or recorded by humans, it often reflects existing societal biases. Bias in data can lead to flawed AI models that reinforce discrimination rather than eliminate it (see Figure 4).

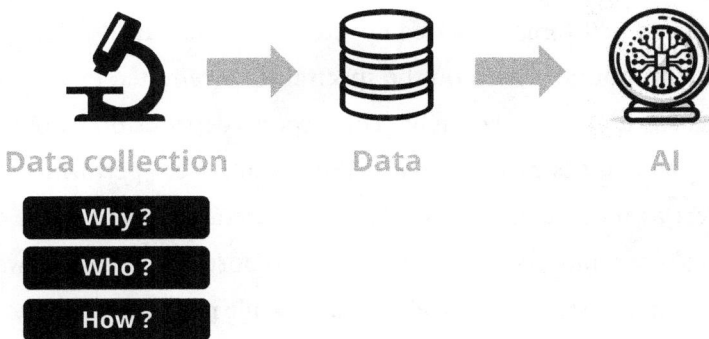

Data collection   Data   AI

Why ?

Who ?

How ?

Figure 4: AI is biased because it is using biased data. Keep in mind that there is no raw data.

Some common types of bias include:

- **Selection bias**: When some groups are systematically over- or underrepresented in a dataset. For example, a poll that offers a gaming console as an incentive might overrepresent young male gamers.

- **Reporting bias**: When certain events are more likely to be documented than others, it can skew the results. For example, when a researcher only selects part of the collected data based on a specific region in the world.

- **Detection bias**: When the probability of observing an event varies based on external factors. For instance, pollution measurements may be biased if sensors are placed only in easily accessible locations, missing heavily polluted areas.

An example comes from a company providing security and track-and-trace solutions to governments. To verify the authenticity of products, customs are equipped with handheld devices. Authentication is based on the spectral signal emitted by the ink in response to a specific light. This process depends on who and how the audit is run. Several measurements were performed to collect as much data as possible. After several weeks of usage of the solution, one of the custom auditors reported problems. It was found that the auditor was left-handed, while most measurements used to build the solution were taken by right-handed people.

Should you let the data speak for itself?

We often hear or read that the data speaks for itself. This means that we as humans should not use our experience or gut feeling to make decisions, but rather trust data. However, this is not as easy as it looks. Indeed, as you have discovered in this chapter, data is always biased (someone collected this data, for specific reasons, in precise ways, etc.) Also, as we will see in Chapter 4, when visualizing data, we decide how to plot it, and this affects the message conveyed by the data. So now if I tell you that the data doesn't lie, you should be suspicious. Being critical about data is a key skill for any decision maker, especially in a time when a significant number of employees use Generative AI in their daily work.

Missing values and outliers

Two important notions about data that you will encounter in your company are missing values and outliers. These concepts are essential for decision-making. Indeed, when data specialists report missing values and outliers, you need to be able to communicate with them about how to proceed, as this depends on your specific use case and domain expertise.

When some data is missing in your dataset, you must think about how to deal with it. Missing values mean that the information was not recorded, available, or was deleted. They can appear as blank in your dataset or have a standard value such as "999" or "NA" for Not Available. For example, in your customer data, you may have missing values for the age column. The decision you take, whether to keep it as is or correct the data, depends on the effort needed and your data quality strategy. Note that removing rows or columns with missing values is usually not the right approach. Indeed, the fact that the data is missing is already information in itself.

Outliers are values that differ from the "normal" behavior. The challenge to detect outliers depends on your definition of what is normal. While there are statistical approaches to detect outliers, the correct treatment is strongly dependent on your business application. The same comments about missing values apply here as well. We will discuss how to process missing values and outliers in Chapter 2.

The issue with correlated features

Data privacy is a complex topic that needs specific attention. A common misconception is that removing sensitive variables like race or gender from datasets eliminates bias. However, correlated features often serve as substitutes. For example, neighborhood data in US cities is highly correlated with race due to historical segregation. AI models trained on such data may still replicate biased outcomes, even if direct indicators of race are absent. Organizations must proactively detect and address these hidden correlations. To mitigate this risk, perform careful feature selection, reflecting on each data column. Next, surround yourself with various domain experts, not only data and IT specialists.

Data versus information

In this book, we consider information as data linked together. As soon as data is joined together, analyzed, or visualized, we consider it as information. Such information can be used to make data-driven decisions for the company.

In a nutshell

This chapter introduced key aspects of data and its role in AI, emphasizing that data is never neutral and must be understood in its context. We also covered methods of collection and common biases. You can keep in mind that:

- **Data is never raw**: Every dataset reflects human decisions—what to measure, how to collect it, and what to exclude. These choices affect the reliability of any AI model built on that data.

- **Existing systems rarely collect the right data for AI**: Operational data may be useful, but it often lacks the structure or coverage needed for AI projects. Additional data collection is frequently necessary.

- **Removing sensitive variables does not remove bias**: Features correlated with variables like race or gender can still carry bias, even if the sensitive attributes themselves are excluded.

Understanding these points helps build better, fairer, and more effective data systems from the start. In the next chapter, we will highlight the importance of data quality for any data-related initiative, whether AI or not.

Do you want to know more?

To learn more about the importance of data and data monetization, read: "Data is everybody's business", "Everydata", and "*People and Data*".

TWO

You Need Quality Data

Data quality has a direct impact on the success of any AI project. Poor-quality data leads to unreliable results, no matter how complex the algorithm. This chapter explains why data quality remains a common issue in companies and how it affects AI performance. It reviews where problems appear in the data pipeline, from collection to storage. Also how AI can assist with data cleaning tasks, such as deduplication and filling in missing values. Through example, it highlights both the risks of ignoring data quality and the benefits of addressing it early in the process.

Why data quality matters

Every decision maker needs to know what it means to work on data quality. Indeed, as you plan to base some of your decisions on data, it is essential to know what kind of decisions you can make and with what level of confidence. You certainly heard the axiom *"garbage in, garbage out"*. This is an excellent way to illustrate the challenges of poor data quality with AI. Indeed, bad data means bad results (see Figure 5).

Bad data   AI   Bad results

Figure 5: AI using bad data will inevitably deliver bad results.

When we mention data quality, this can have a different meaning for people. In this book, we define data quality as the process of evaluating and improving the quality of existing datasets within the company. In each dataset, specific data can be:

- Missing (not available)
- An outlier (far from the "normal" data)
- Duplicated (repeated two or more times)
- Invalid (not satisfying business rules)

The first two examples have been discussed in the last chapter. The third one will be discussed later in this chapter. For an example of invalid data, imagine a customer at an age younger than the time since becoming a client. This does not make sense and can be captured with a business rule.

Measuring and improving data quality is a vast domain. Here are examples of data quality topics:

- **Data profiling**: Assessing the structure and quality of data to identify inconsistencies.

- **Matching**: Finding and merging duplicate records using rules or algorithms (more about deduplication with a concrete example later in this chapter).

- **Geocoding**: Standardizing location-based data to improve consistency.

- **Enrichment**: Enhancing data completeness with external sources.

Figure 6 is an example of how the company Nestlé can be written in the different systems of another company (ERP, CRM, etc.).

Company name
Nestlé
Nestle
NESTLE
NESTLÉ
Néstle
Nestl
...

Figure 6: Example of a company name written with a different spelling in the same database.

> **Data quality is key**
>
> If you want to deep dive into the topic of data quality, read the various articles by Tom Redman, such as "How to Make Everyone Great at Data" in Harvard Business Review.

As a decision maker, you need to understand why data quality is not easily solved within companies. Indeed, companies often struggle with data quality due to several challenges:

- The increasing volume of data makes it harder to manage and clean.
- Data comes in diverse formats, making integration complex.
- Access to domain experts, who can validate data, is limited.
- Documentation is often outdated or missing.
- Data quality is often not a priority for top management.

To overcome these issues, businesses must not only treat data as a strategic asset but also treat data quality as a key focus area. What is even more crucial is to understand the complementarity of what Tom Redman in "Ensure High-Quality Data Powers Your AI" calls "right data" and "data is right". To solve a given challenge, you need the right data. You may have data, but it's still not the right data to solve your specific use case. Second, that data (when it is the right one) must be right. This means with a high enough level of quality. This can be summarized by the idea of "fitness for use" of the data, which means the data is of sufficient quality, relevance, and reliability.

Companies struggle with data quality for several reasons. One of the key reasons is that data quality is often not a priority for top management. This is due to various reasons. First, top management may not have (yet) a data-driven mindset. Second, the return on investment of data quality initiatives is sometimes challenging to measure, especially in the short term. Third, everybody wants to lead the fancy AI topic, but who wants to work on painful data quality? However, as written in Evan Stubbs' "Delivering Business Analytics":

Blaming bad data never justifies inaction.

Case study: deduplication of hotel data

Most of the data you will use in your company has some duplicates. Therefore, having a view on how to remove duplicates is important. Note that while we clean data before doing AI, AI can also be used to improve data quality. To illustrate this, consider the challenge of deduplicating hotel records in a large online travel platform. This issue has a direct impact on user experience and system performance.

When users search for a hotel, the platform should ideally show a single, accurate listing. However, due to data being collected from various sources, each with its own formatting and naming conventions, duplicate entries are common. One hotel might appear as "Hotel Podium" in one dataset and "Podium Hotel" in another, with slight differences in address or amenities. These duplicates distort analytics and mislead end users, whether within the company or customers (see Figure 7).

Missing character

Source #1	Source #2
Hotel Podium	Hotel Pdium

Word order

Source #1	Source #2
Hotel Podium Barcelona	Hotel Barcelona Podium

Different words

Source #1	Source #2
Hotel NH Podium Barcelona	Hotel NH Podium

Figure 7: Examples of duplicate hotels because of missing characters, word order, and different words.

To solve this, an AI model can be trained to identify duplicate entries. The approach is based on fuzzy matching of text. Rather than relying on exact matches, the algorithm compares strings in a flexible way, recognizing similarities even when names or addresses are slightly different. Additional features, such as geographic location and further hotel information, can also be used to improve accuracy.

In one case, applying this technique reduced the duplicates by a double-digit percentage, significantly improving the platform's data quality. Importantly, this also streamlined the customer journey and reduced operational costs related to manual data cleaning. This was performed on hotel data, but it can be applied to customer, supplier, and employee data as well. This example highlights that AI can be used to improve data quality, in this case, reducing duplicate entries.

Where to address data quality issues

Data quality problems can appear at multiple stages of the data pipeline. To be able to lead data initiatives effectively and allocate your teams accordingly, let's review where challenges can be solved:

- **At the source**: Errors can be introduced when data is collected, whether manually or automatically.

- **During processing**: Data transformations, merging, and cleaning steps can introduce inconsistencies.

- **In storage**: Data warehouses and lakes may contain duplicate or conflicting records.

Addressing data quality early at the source reduces the effort required to fix issues later. Of course, this will have a short-term higher cost. However, correcting the data quality issue at the source is beneficial for your company in the long term (see Figure 8).

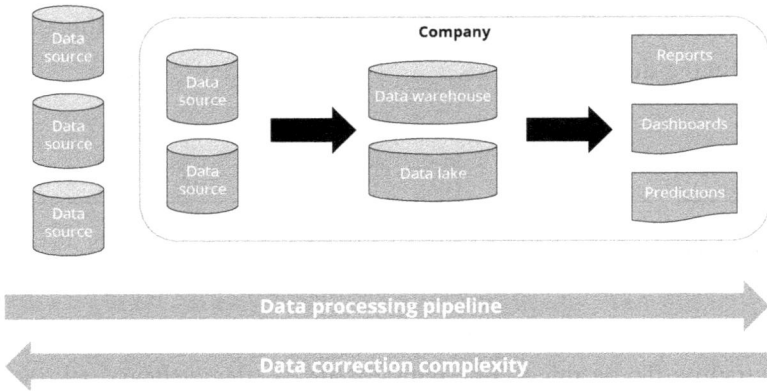

Figure 8: Addressing data quality challenges sooner in the data processing pipeline is better, but more complex, as more stakeholders and data source systems are involved.

Data quality is part of a broader effort to manage data in a company, which is referred to as data governance. The DAMA-DMBOK defines data governance as:

> *[...] the exercise of authority and control (planning, monitoring, and enforcement) over the management of data assets.*

As a decision maker, you need to know that while data governance is a needed initiative, it does not guarantee the success of data quality. Data quality is so important that it deserves specific focus and attention from various stakeholders in the company. For more information about data governance, you can read "Non-Invasive Data Governance" by Robert Steiner.

Improving data quality

Improving data quality is a continuous effort. Here are a few key steps so that you can decide when to spend effort and when you can move on with your data initiatives:

- **Start with what you have**: Assess the current state of data quality and set realistic expectations. Perfect data does not exist, so focus on incremental improvements.

- **Ask the right questions**: Why do quality issues exist (where do they originate)? What actions can be taken to clean the data? How do these issues impact business decisions?

- **Use AI to improve data quality**: AI models can help detect anomalies, clean datasets, and fill missing values using data imputation techniques.

AI to improve data quality

We often consider data quality as the first step before using AI algorithms. It is key to also consider AI as a way to improve data quality. Knowing this can help you assign some of your data scientists[2] to improve data quality. For example, AI can be used to detect outliers and impute missing values, among others. To go deeper, check the article "*Deploying machine learning based data quality controls – Design principles and insights from the field*".

---

[2] I will discuss more about the role of Data Scientists in Chapter 8.

In a nutshell

This chapter explained why data quality is essential for AI success and how companies can both prevent and fix quality issues using concrete methods.

- **Data quality is key**: No (good) data, no (good) AI. Recognizing the importance of good quality data is the best starting point for any of your data and AI initiatives.
- **AI can help improve data quality**: In the hotel deduplication case, an AI model using fuzzy matching improved duplicate detection, showing that AI is not only a user but also a contributor to better data.
- **Addressing issues at the source is ideal in the long-term**: Fixing problems early in the pipeline reduces downstream errors and is valuable to your company in the long-term.

Improving data quality is not a one-time fix but a long-term investment that directly impacts the success of AI projects. In the next chapter we will discuss the importance of summary statistics to better understand your data.

Do you want to know more?

In case you want to deep dive into the topic of data quality, and more broadly data governance, you can read the following books: "*Non-Invasive Data Governance*", "*Making data governance work*", and "*Data Management Body of Knowledge*" (DAMA-DMBOK).

THREE

Summary Statistics Wanted

Summary statistics help to make sense of large datasets by showing key characteristics such as central tendency and variability. This chapter explains the main statistical measures, including mean, median, and standard deviation, and when to use each one. It also covers more advanced tools like correlation and principal component analysis to reveal trends in the data. Common errors in interpretation are discussed, including the confusion between correlation and causation. Finally, the chapter highlights the limitations of summary statistics and the importance of data visualization in avoiding misleading conclusions.

The power of summary statistics

Summary statistics condense large datasets into manageable insights. As a decision maker, you are confronted with these statistics regularly. It is thus crucial that you understand what they mean and their limits. The most common ones include:

- **Mean (Average)**: The sum of all values divided by the number of observations. It provides a general idea of central tendency but is sensitive to outliers.

- **Median**: The middle value when data is ordered. Unlike the mean, it is robust to extreme values, making it more reliable when distributions are skewed.

- **Min/Max**: The smallest and largest values in a dataset, indicating the range of variation.

- **Standard Deviation**: Measures data dispersion around the mean. A high standard deviation suggests significant variability, while a low one indicates stability.

The distinction between the mean and median is crucial, especially in skewed distributions. This is important for you to know, as you may draw different conclusions depending on the results of the statistics. You should consider asking for both of them when you only see one. As an example, consider US household income: the mean is significantly higher than the median due to a few extremely high incomes. Relying on the mean alone would give a misleading picture of economic reality. The median, being less influenced by outliers, offers a more accurate representation of a typical household's income.

When sharing insights with business stakeholders, it is key to be clear and persuasive. Metrics like the median are slightly more complex to explain than the mean. Therefore, we advise using either the mean or the median, depending on the context, the data literacy of stakeholders, and the specific dataset concerned.

Visualizing summary statistics

Graphical representations, such as boxplots, help interpret summary statistics effectively. As a decision maker, you are exposed to such plots when reading technical reports. A boxplot displays:

- Minimum and maximum values
- First and third quartiles (25th and 75th percentiles)
- Median (50th percentile).

Figure 9 shows an example with the height distribution of people (illustrative dataset). This visualization enables quick comparisons and outlier detection, facilitating better data-driven decisions.

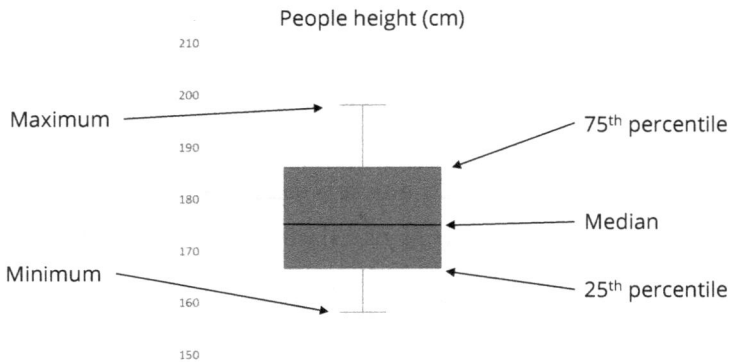

Figure 9: Illustration of the box plot with people's heights.

Further data visualizations

Data visualization will be detailed further in Chapter 4. You can refer to the following books to study how to leverage statistics to understand your data: "Stats with Cats" and "Naked Statistics".

Correlation and PCA

While summary statistics provide essential insights, additional statistical methods can uncover deeper trends. While you do not need to know the details of the approaches below, it will give you a better understanding of what data scientists are working with as statistical techniques:

- **Pearson's correlation coefficient**: Measures the linear relationship between two variables (see Figure 10), ranging from -1 (perfect negative correlation) to +1 (perfect positive correlation). It is vital to keep in mind that correlation does not imply causation (this is discussed later in the chapter).

- **Principal Component Analysis (PCA)**: A technique that reduces data complexity by transforming correlated variables into uncorrelated principal components. PCA is valuable for visualization and dimensionality reduction in AI.

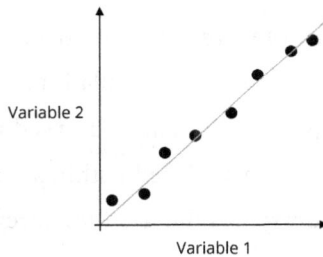

Figure 10: Linear correlation is close to 1 between variables 1 and 2.

Regarding correlation, as explained in "Stats with Cats":

If you find that your predictor variables [input] are highly correlated with your dependent variable [output], that's great.

Indeed, this means that there are trends in the data that you can use to predict the output, using your input variables. We will discuss more about input and output variables in Chapter 5.

Correlation and PCA

If you are curious about correlation and PCA, and want to understand statistics and data science better, check the book "Introduction to Data Mining".

Common pitfalls and misinterpretations

To make an informed decision when confronted with statistics, you need to know that they can be misleading when used improperly. Some common issues include:

- **Over-reliance on the mean**: Without considering data distribution, the mean can distort reality.
- **Ignoring sample size**: Averages from small samples may not represent the overall population.
- **Simpson's paradox**: Trends observed in aggregated data may reverse when analyzed within subgroups. This paradox underscores the need for careful segmentation in analysis.

When possible, use a combination of absolute values and percentages. Indeed, we often use percentages to allow easier comparison between different groups. However, we should always keep in mind the size of our groups (visible with the absolute values). Therefore, when calculating statistics or plotting your data, try to show both the absolute values and corresponding percentages.

The case of correlation

A major challenge with correlation is that it is often interpreted as causation or at least a strong connection. As a decision maker, you need to be aware of this to avoid drawing incorrect conclusions for your business. These are two significant issues with correlations:

- **Correlation versus causation**: It is human nature to try to find a causal effect when two variables are correlated. It has been shown that chocolate consumption is significantly correlated with the number of Nobel laureates at a country level.[3] However, in this case, there is likely an external factor connecting the two.

- **Spurious correlations**: Coincidental relationships may appear statistically significant but lack connection. This is because we collect more and more data. Therefore, it is easy to find two variables that are correlated by chance. Check the *spurious correlations* website[4] to discover absurd but statistically valid correlations.

Ice creams and sharks

The relationship between ice cream sales and shark attacks can illustrate another example of the correlation versus causation issue. These two variables are highly correlated. However, unlike what some people expected, selling more ice cream does not cause more shark attacks (and the same is true the other way round). There is a third variable making the link: the season (or temperature). Indeed, we sell more ice cream in summer and more shark attacks are reported in summer.

---

[3] Check the article "Chocolate consumption and Noble laureates".

[4] www.tylervigen.com/spurious-correlations.

A few words on outliers

While outliers can be detected using statistical approaches, the real question about them is business driven. Decision makers need to support data teams in processing outliers, as this will impact the data-driven decisions. There are three things to keep in mind about outliers in the data:

- **Why?** Try to understand why they are present in the data. Most people remove outliers when they find them. However, if they were present in the data you collected, they are likely to appear again in the future.

- **What?** Defining what an outlier is depends on your application. We may have different views on which data points are outliers in the very same dataset.

- **How?** Choosing the best action to take on a given outlier situation is case dependent. It goes from status quo, to remove the data point (row) or variable (column), to data imputation (see below).

While several statistical approaches exist to detect outliers, the key question remains about the threshold: How many of the abnormal data points do you consider as outliers? One way to answer this question is by asking another one: How many outliers can you investigate?

Imagine you are using an outlier detection algorithm for highlighting fraud cases in a bank. One way to set the threshold on the number of outliers is to set it to the number of cases that the compliance team can investigate. So, as written in "Stats with Cats" by Charles Kufs:

> *They [outliers] may mean nothing so that you can delete them from the analysis, or they may be critical to your interpretation of the dataset.*

Data imputation

In case your dataset has missing values, data imputation may be the right solution. Data imputation means replacing specific values in your dataset with a good estimate. Of course, all the challenge lies in what a good value is. The most common imputation for a numerical variable is the mean or median. If we take the example of customer age, each missing value would be replaced by the median of the age (from where it is available). Just keep in mind that this is also adding noise to your dataset since this is artificial data. You have to consider each case specifically to decide how to proceed.

Summary statistics are not enough

Summary statistics are a good starting point and a powerful way to summarize a dataset. However, as the name suggests, it only summarizes a dataset with potentially hundreds of thousands of rows into a few numbers. Look at the four datasets in Figure 11 and try to guess what they share in common.

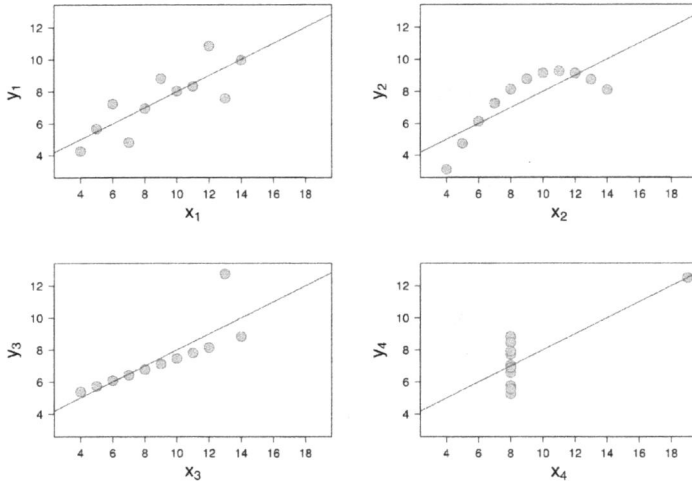

Figure 11: Anscombe Quartet: the four datasets have similar mean and standard deviation for x and the same for y (source: Wikipedia).

These four datasets share the same mean and standard deviation for X and the same for Y. However, looking at the above scatterplot, you will agree that they are quite different. This is a good example that illustrates the importance of data visualization in complementing summary statistics. To make effective decisions, you need to understand this complementarity between statistics and data visualization. Always ask for both; do not be satisfied with only one side of the coin. We will cover the topic of data visualization in the next chapter.

Statistics is broader than the summary statistics we discussed as a way to get information about our data. It is used to provide real-world interpretation to parameters and coefficients. Statistics also provide tools and methods to make conclusions about a larger population, based on data collected from a sample.

In a nutshell

This chapter introduces key summary statistics and their limitations, highlighting the need to go beyond averages for a more insightful understanding.

- **Median is more robust than mean**: In skewed distributions like US household income, the median gives a more accurate view of the typical case than the mean, which can be distorted by outliers.

- **Same statistics, different stories**: The Anscombe Quartet shows that datasets can have identical means and standard deviations yet be visually and structurally different, stressing the importance of data visualization.

- **Outlier management is context-dependent**: Whether to remove or keep an outlier depends on why it is present, what it represents, and how much capacity stakeholders have to investigate it.

Summary statistics are a good first step, but to make the right decisions, you need to understand what is behind the numbers. In the next chapter, we will show the power and challenges of data visualization, which is complementary to summary statistics.

Do you want to know more?

If you are interested by the topic of statistics, excellent introduction books are "Statistics Done Wrong", "*Naked Statistics*", and "*Factfulness*".

FOUR

The Art of Data Visualization

Data visualization is a key step in any data project. It helps explore trends, communicate results, and simplify complex ideas. This chapter explains how to create clear and effective visuals by choosing the right chart, removing clutter, and focusing attention. It presents common mistakes to avoid and principles that guide how people read visuals. The chapter also highlights the difference between exploring data for analysis and presenting it to an audience. Practical advice and examples show how to design visuals that support understanding and good decisions.

Why visualize data?

Most of the data you access as a decision maker is through visuals. This could be in a report, a dashboard, or directly in your emails.

It is of utmost importance to be able to read (and create, when needed) data visualization correctly. As written by Darrell Huff in "How to Lie with Statistics":

> When numbers in tabular form are taboo and words will
> not do the work well, as is often the case,
> there is one answer left: draw a picture.

Data visualization is vital for three main reasons (see Figure 12):

- To **explore** data and identify trends and outliers.
- To **explain** results clearly and persuasively to an audience.
- To **entertain**, making ideas accessible and entertaining to a broader public.

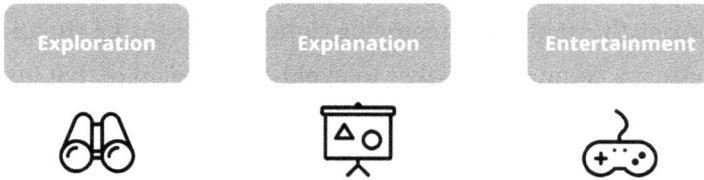

Figure 12: The three main reasons to visualize data.

Knowing why we need a visualization will help us design it in an effective way. Of course, regardless of the purpose, clarity remains key. And as noted by Alberto Cairo in "How Charts Lie":

> Charts may lie, then, because they display either the
> wrong information or too little information. However, a
> chart can show the right type and amount of information
> and lie anyway due to poor design or labeling.

Reading visuals: tips and tricks

When you read and create data visualizations, keep in mind the recommendations below. Understanding visuals is as important as creating them. Some common mistakes can seriously mislead interpretation. Have a look at Figure 13 and think about what is wrong with it.

US Smartphone Marketshare

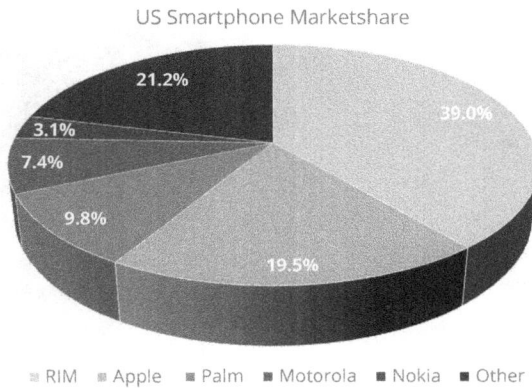

Figure 13: US Smartphone market share (Steve Jobs talk, 2008). What is wrong with this chart?

As you can see in the above picture, it is challenging to compare numbers. Also, the 3D effect is misleading the reader (Apple's market share looks bigger than the "other" category). First, our brain is not good at comparing angles. Therefore, pie charts and donut charts are not the optimal way to display information. When possible, use bar charts instead. As written in Cole Nussbaumer Knaflic's "Storytelling with Data":

There are also some specific graph types and elements that you should avoid: pie charts, donut charts, 3D, and secondary y-axes.

Rule #1 – Avoid pie and donut charts

Now, look at the Figure 14. What is wrong with it?

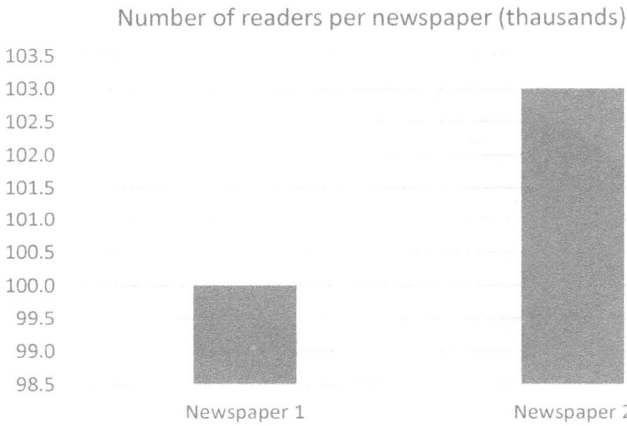

Number of readers per newspaper (thausands)

103.5	
103.0	
102.5	
102.0	
101.5	
101.0	
100.5	
100.0	
99.5	
99.0	
98.5	
Newspaper 1	Newspaper 2

Figure 14: Example of a bar chart. What is wrong with it?

It appears that Newspaper 2 is sold three times more than Newspaper 1. Now look at the left axis. This is one of the most common ways to cheat in data visualization: the bar chart doesn't start at zero. The challenge is that our brains always try to compare the bars, so not starting at zero gives the impression of a bigger difference than reality.

Rule #2 – Start bar charts at zero

Let's have a look at Figure 15. What is wrong with it?

Composition of a food product (percentage)

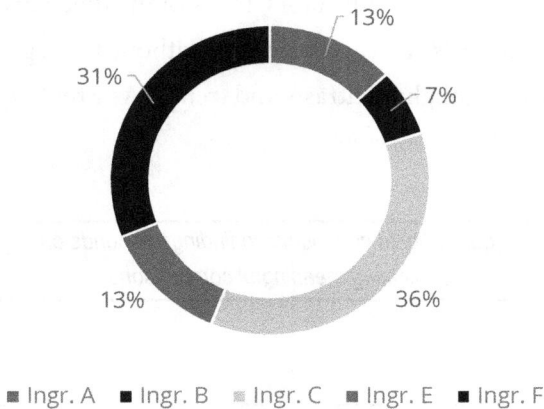

■ Ingr. A   ■ Ingr. B   ▨ Ingr. C   ■ Ingr. E   ■ Ingr. F

Figure 15: Example of a donut chart. What is wrong with it?

It looks like some ingredients belong to the same group, since the same color is used. With the available information, these "groups" don't make sense. Keep in mind that colors encode information. For example, light versus dark may mean low versus high. Also, red may mean danger or negative values. Try to use consistent colors to avoid confusion, especially in dashboards, as there are several plots. Also, keep in mind people who are color-blind (with a non-optimal combination, such as red-green).

Rule #3 – Use colors wisely

We propose other advice, such as avoiding 3D effects. One thing that strikes is the difficulty in reading these charts. Indeed, it is hard to compare numbers with perspective effects. These effects must be avoided at all costs.

Also, try to make comparisons as easy as possible. For example, when showing a map with colors, think of the link between colors and how easy it is to read the visual without the legend. Charts must clearly highlight contrasts and trends. As Brent Dykes writes in "Effective Data Storytelling":

Your ability to communicate findings depends on facilitating meaningful comparisons.

Know your audience

Before opening your preferred data visualization tool, such as Tableau, PowerBI, or even Excel, take a moment to think about your audience (see Figure 16). When you help other people make decisions based on your work, you need to ask yourself several questions: What matters to them? What is their expertise? What questions may they have? These are useful questions to ask yourself before designing your slides and visuals. You can also go deeper with inclusive topics related to color blindness.

Figure 16: Typical questions to ask yourself before designing slides and visuals.

Creating effective visuals

Designing good charts is not only about software skills. It is about choosing the correct chart, removing unnecessary elements, and guiding the reader's focus (Figure 17). Knowing these tips will help you create more effective visualizations.

Figure 17: Three key steps for compelling visuals: choose the right visualization, remove clutter, and focus attention.

- **Choose the right visualization**: Start by identifying the best category of plots (comparison, distribution, or relationship). Then, select the best chart type (for example, "scatterplot" or "bubble chart"). Eventually, fine-tune the options (axes, colors, etc.).

- **Remove clutter**: Eliminate all clutter unless it adds value. Try to think of the ink-to-information ratio: is there any clutter (ink) you can remove while keeping clear the main message (information)?

- **Focus attention**: Use pre-attentive attributes (size, color, position) to direct attention where it matters. Anything to help your audience focus will make your visualization clearer and more impactful. Remember, you should do the job to make the information easily accessible to your audience.

Let's do a quick exercise to illustrate the usefulness of focusing attention. Look at the left part of Figure 18 (only the left part). How many "7" do you count? Now, look at the picture on the right. How many "7" do you count? This is the power of focusing attention using pre-attentive attributes (like color).

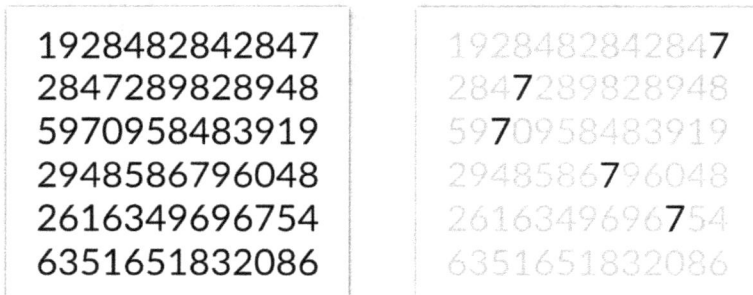

1928482842847	1928482842847
2847289828948	2847289828948
5970958483919	5970958483919
2948586796048	2948586796048
2616349696754	2616349696754
6351651832086	6351651832086

Figure 18: Look at the picture on the left: how many "7" do you count? Now, look at the picture on the right. How many "7" do you count? This is the power of pre-attentive attributes.

Another key principle in data visualization to keep in mind, is that perfection is not when there is nothing left to add to the visual, but when there is nothing left to take away from it.

Imagine you create a line chart with monthly sales of your company for the last five years. Do you need to show decimal values? Should you have the value displayed close to each point on the graph? Do you need each month in full text?

How to encode information

There are many ways to encode information in a visual. Have a look at Figure 19. According to it, do you think it is easier to read information on the left or right side? Usually information is easier to read on the right side. This does not mean that colors shouldn't be used. Just keep in mind that colors may be interpreted differently, and about 4.5% of the world population has some form of color blindness.[5]

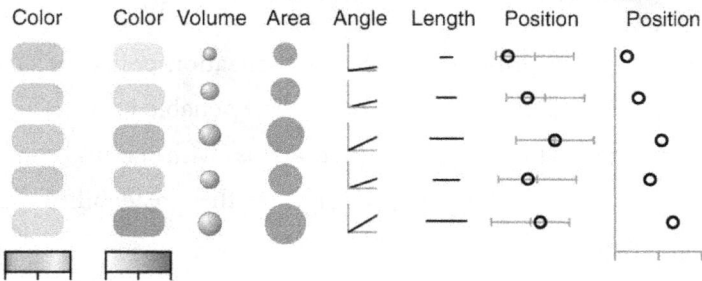

Figure 19: Different ways to encode information (Source: Design of data figures (B. Wong), Nature Methods (2010), https://doi.org/10.1038/nmeth0910-665).

Our brains interpret visual information using intuitive rules known as Gestalt principles. These principles help us quickly and naturally organize visual elements, making them especially useful in the design of dashboards, reports, and other data visualizations. Key principles include:

- **Proximity**: Elements that are close to each other are perceived as a group.

---

[5] www.colourblindawareness.org/colour-blindness.

- **Similarity**: Items that share visual characteristics, such as shape or color, are seen as related.
- **Enclosure**: Objects within a bounded area are understood as belonging together.
- **Closure**: The mind tends to fill in missing parts of a visual to perceive a complete form.
- **Continuity**: The eye is drawn along paths, lines, or curves, even when they are interrupted.
- **Connection**: Elements that are visually connected (by a line or arrow) are interpreted as related.

Applying these principles in data visualization enhances clarity and guides user attention effectively. They enable information to be structured in a manner that aligns with natural human perception, thereby improving both readability and comprehension.

While you don't need to think about all these principles for each visual you design, it is good practice to take a few of them and challenge your existing plots.

Data storytelling

People do not believe in numbers; they believe in a story. While this is a bit provocative, my point is that the story around your data is crucial. As a decision maker, you need to keep that in mind to tell an impactful data story.

Not all visuals serve the same purpose. Some are exploratory, used by data professionals to make sense of the data. Others are explanatory, used to communicate findings. You will start by generating several visuals to explore your data. Most of these graphs won't tell an interesting story. Still, you have to create them to discover that. Once done, interesting graphs are selected and then put together as a story (Figure 20).

Figure 20: We start by generating several visuals while exploring the data. We then select interesting plot(s). Eventually, we refine the plot(s) to tell a story.

As suggested by Brent Dykes in "Effective Data Storytelling", imagine you are Indiana Jones. You are both an archaeologist (exploring the data) and a professor (explaining that data). A successful data story combines facts, visuals, and narrative. It connects with the audience and leads to better decisions.

Homework

Next time you see a visual in a newspaper, on TV, or on your favorite social media, ask yourself the following questions: What is the main message? Is it the right chart? Is the comparison clear?

In a nutshell

This chapter highlighted the role of data visualization in exploring, explaining, and communicating complex ideas clearly and effectively.

- **Pie and donut charts often mislead**: Our brain struggles with angles and areas, making bar charts a better option for comparing values accurately.

- **Three key steps to effective visualizations**: Select the right chart (start top-down), remove clutter (anything useless), and focus attention (help your audience read visuals).

- **Separate exploration with explanation**: You have to start with exploring your data, therefore creating plenty of plots. Then you need to explain the plots, telling a story to your audience. These are two different jobs.

Visuals are powerful tools, but only when they are designed with purpose, clarity, and your audience in mind. Now let's move from data to AI.

Do you want to know more?

In case you are curious about the topic, here are interesting resources to improve your data visualization skills: "How Charts Lie", "*Storytelling with Data*", and "*Effective Data Storytelling*". If you want to go more technical, you can try "*Visualize This*" and "Data Visualization".

FIVE

Machines That Learn

Understanding AI requires clear definitions of its main terms and methods. This chapter introduces key concepts, including big data, statistics, data science, and machine learning. It explains the differences between supervised and unsupervised learning, and describes popular techniques such as clustering and decision trees. Real-world examples show how machine learning models are built, evaluated, and used in business. The chapter also highlights common challenges such as data leakage, overfitting, and the balance between accuracy and business value. These foundations are essential for any AI project.

Key definitions in AI

Understanding the terminology behind AI is essential for decision makers to communicate effectively with various data and IT teams. While buzzwords evolve rapidly, the foundational concepts remain consistent. This chapter provides definitions of the most frequently used terms in the field, demystifying their meanings and highlighting their roles in business and technology.

Big data

Big data refers to datasets so large or complex that traditional data processing tools cannot manage them effectively. It is commonly characterized by the 3Vs:[6]

- **Volume**: The sheer amount of data.
- **Variety**: The different forms of data (text, image, video).
- **Velocity**: The speed at which data is generated and processed.

The meaning of big data here is the idea of developing specific infrastructure to store and manage large-scale information efficiently. Nowadays, most big data systems are running on cloud environments.

How useful is your "big data"? It is not because you have access to a "big data" environment with a vast amount of data that you have the right data for your use case. Keep in mind that most existing systems, machines, and processes were coded a long time ago, and without any specific wish to use AI on top of the data collected.

---

[6] Proposed by Doug Laney in his article "3-D Data Management: Controlling Data Volume, Velocity and Variety".

For example, I worked on a project for an audit using machine learning. While the available amount of data was huge, most of it was usernames with timestamps. This may be little data to perform AI, whatever the volume.

Statistics

Statistics is a branch of mathematics that involves collecting, analyzing, and interpreting data. It is rooted in the hypothesize-and-test approach. A key assumption is that data follows a known stochastic[7] model. Statistics is particularly useful when the objective is to confirm or reject hypotheses with a controlled methodology. See Chapter 3 for more information.

Data mining and data science

Data mining is the process of uncovering trends or knowledge from large datasets. It is described as the *"non-trivial extraction of implicit, previously unknown, and potentially useful information"*.[8] Over time, the term Data Science has largely replaced Data Mining, reflecting a broader and more business-oriented scope. Data science integrates data understanding, value creation, and communication, making it a cornerstone for modern analytics initiatives. More about the data science process in Chapter 8.

---

[7] In statistics, stochastic means something that involves randomness or chance.

[8] Check the article "Knowledge Discovery in Databases: An Overview".

Statistics versus data science

As defined in the Oxford dictionary, "*Statistics is a branch of mathematics working with data collection, organization, analysis, interpretation and presentation*". Statistics is based on the hypothesis-and-test approach. You first make a hypothesis and then test it with data. Data science, on the other hand, starts with analyzing the data to find meaningful patterns. While this is the official distinction, today statistics and data science are often used interchangeably. For more information on this topic, you can read the article "Statistical modeling: the two cultures."

Artificial Intelligence (AI)

The field of AI has existed since the 1950s. The primary goal of AI is to replicate human intelligence with a computer. The concept of intelligent machines dates to the 1950s, when Alan Turing proposed the famous "Turing Test" (1950) as a way to measure machine intelligence. The term "Artificial Intelligence" was first coined by John McCarthy at the Dartmouth Conference in 1956, which is often considered the official birth of the field.

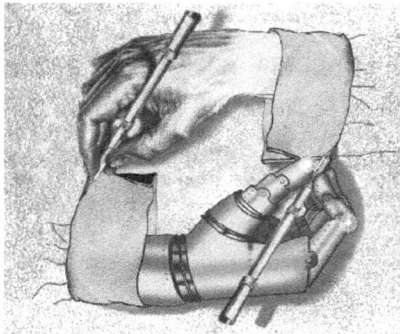

Figure 21: The human teaches the machine (i.e., the computer) how to learn.
Original image is "Drawing Hands" by M.C. Escher, 1948.

Figure 21 is an interesting representation of a human hand drawing a mechanical hand, itself drawing the human hand. I like to interpret it as a human-AI interaction to learn from each other.

Machine learning

Machine Learning (ML) is a subfield of AI, enabling computers to learn from data. It focuses on pattern discovery rather than hypothesis testing. While data science looks at the entire value chain of data, machine learning focuses on algorithm development and optimization. We discuss machine learning in more detail later in this chapter.

Deep learning

Deep Learning is a subfield of machine learning that uses artificial neural networks with many layers to learn patterns from large amounts of data. It has become especially effective in tasks such as image recognition and natural language processing. Deep learning systems can learn complex representations from raw data, making them highly versatile. If you are interested about deep learning, read the book, "Codeless Deep Learning with KNIME".

Natural Language Processing (NLP)

In today's data-driven world, a vast majority of corporate data is unstructured. This includes text documents, emails, social media posts, and call transcripts. Natural Language Processing (NLP) is a branch of AI that focuses on giving computers the ability to understand, interpret, and generate human language. Companies that succeed in leveraging unstructured data can gain a strong competitive advantage. NLP enables them to do so. We will provide concrete examples of NLP in the chapter on Generative AI.

Generative AI

Generative AI models, such as those behind ChatGPT, are designed to create new content—text, images, or other media—based on trends learned from data. These models can produce novel outputs rather than merely classifying or predicting. A well-known example is the use of Large Language Models (LLMs), which generate human-like text by predicting sequences of words. Generative AI is detailed in Chapter 7.

AI Agents

AI agents refer to systems capable of making autonomous decisions and taking actions toward complex goals. These systems operate with minimal supervision and often rely on LLMs for decision-making. The automation of tasks using agents marks a step forward in operational efficiency and autonomy. Still, do not expect miracles, as noted in "Agentic Artificial Intelligence":

> *One of the most striking limitations of AI agents is their*
> *lack of common-sense reasoning.*

We discuss AI agents further in Chapter 9.

Artificial General Intelligence (AGI)

AGI, often called *"strong AI"*, refers to machines that can perform any intellectual task that a human can. Unlike current systems, which are designed for specific tasks (known as *"narrow AI"*), AGI aims to replicate the full range of human cognitive abilities. Today, all applications fall under the umbrella of narrow AI. We discuss the limits of AI further in Chapter 9. As written in "Artificial Unintelligence" by Meredith Broussard:

> *[...] general AI is what we want [...]. Narrow AI is what we*
> *have.*

Is AGI coming (soon)?

This question has been subject to discussion for decades already. Even among key AI leaders, opinions can be divergent. People predicted the end of humanity to happen... well, several times already. While I won't speculate about the time AGI will take place (or even if it will) in this book, I still want to emphasize the fact that the sum of (many) narrow AIs is not making anything close to AGI. While machine learning and deep learning are areas with high focus nowadays, there is no guarantee that this is the right path to AGI, as we will see in Chapter 9.

A gentle introduction to machine learning

When using AI to make decisions for your company, you need to know how it works. This will help you envision the possibilities of AI and also be aware of the related limits and what should not be expected from AI.

AI refers to the broader goal of creating machines capable of performing tasks that would typically require human intelligence. When AI is performed by learning from data, it is referred to as machine learning. A further subset, deep learning, refers to algorithms based on neural networks with many layers of neurons. Generative AI is a subfield of deep learning, focusing on generating new content, having learned the data distribution. Figure 22 shows how these key concepts appeared in history.

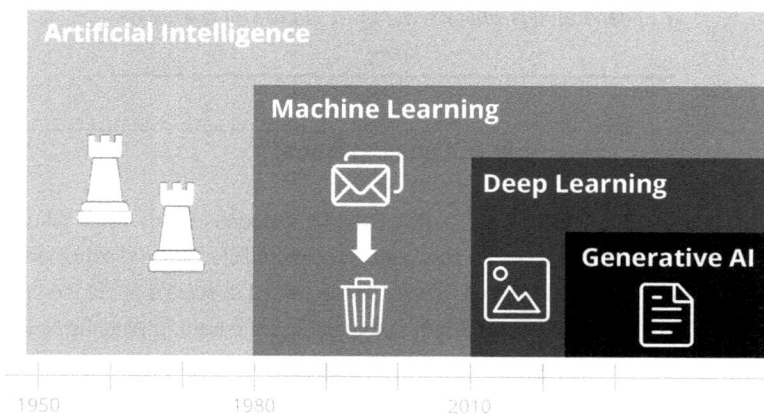

Figure 22: The distinction between four key concepts: AI, Machine Learning, Deep Learning, and Generative AI.

Types of machine learning models

Machine learning models can be categorized into three broad types (Figure 23), each serving different business needs:

- **Descriptive Models**: Help understand data by identifying patterns such as clusters or anomalies. Examples include customer segmentation or fraud detection.

- **Predictive Models**: Predict or forecast future outcomes based on existing data. This includes predicting sales, estimating customer churn,[9] or anticipating machine failure.

- **Generative Models**: Create new data based on existing patterns. These models are used in various applications, including text generation, image creation, and music composition.

Descriptive	Predictive	Generative
Clustering, outlier detection, etc.	Prediction, forecasting, etc.	Text generation, image creation, etc.

Figure 23: Three complementary approaches: description, prediction, and generation.

---

[9] In simple terms, customer churning (or attrition) means the ones leaving the company (for example cancelling a subscription).

These types of models are not mutually exclusive. In practice, they complement each other by providing a complete analytical framework. While generative approaches will be discussed in Chapter 7, we will now cover descriptive (unsupervised learning) and predictive (supervised learning) approaches.

How do machines learn?

As a decision maker, you may be used to what I call "traditional programming". It is key to understanding how this differs from machine learning so you can understand what is needed for these systems to work properly. In traditional programming, rules (programs) are manually coded by a human in the "if-then-else" logic. It takes some input data and computes the desired output. This works well in all cases where you know how to write the program to solve the problem.

Now, if I ask you to write a program to detect a car in a picture, that would be impossible. Even if you were able to do it, I would give you a new picture, and your program would not work anymore. In such situations, when it is too hard or impossible to manually code the program, we can try the machine learning approach. Deciding when to use (or not) machine learning is a challenging task. In Figure 24, we provide examples of insights when ML may be a good idea or not.

ML may work well	ML may not work well
Impossible to write the program for a human	Predictable answers are important
Too much data to analyze for a human	Understanding and explainability are desired
Relationships within the data are too complex for a human	Reproducibility is needed
A lot of data is available	No or little data is available

Figure 24: Examples where Machine Learning (ML) may (or may not) work well. This helps you decide if it is suitable for your specific case.

In machine learning, the paradigm is different: you provide input and desired output to the computer, which computes the program for you. For example, you provide several pictures of images (input) for which you also provide a label, for example, whether there is a car in the image (output). With the appropriate algorithm, the computer can generate a model (a program) to detect cars in images (see Figure 25).

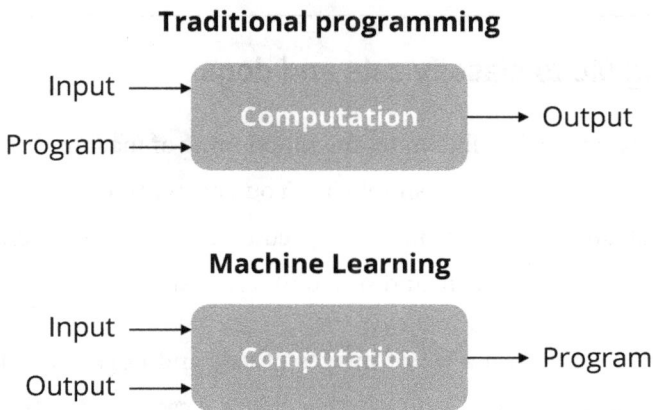

Traditional programming

Input ⟶ [Computation] ⟶ Output
Program ⟶

Machine Learning

Input ⟶ [Computation] ⟶ Program
Output ⟶

Figure 25: Two complementary approaches to solving a problem: traditional programming and machine learning.

There are many conditions for this to work properly, such as the quantity of labeled data, the quality of these data, the presence of learnable patterns, and the choice of the machine learning algorithm. We will discuss these points in this chapter and the following ones.

This book is not about specific tools or languages to perform machine learning. While you may not be the one developing the solutions, be aware of the various options to do so. I can mention two key programming languages used nowadays: Python and R.[10] A variety of no-code (or low-code) tools are also available (paid or free), such as SAS, SPSS, Dataiku, Alteryx, and KNIME. In case you prefer cloud platforms, Microsoft, AWS, and Google also provide specific environments for machine learning development and deployment.

Using ML to classify cats and dogs

The example below illustrates the functioning of machine learning with cats and dogs, for simplicity. You can replace cat/dog with any categories you find helpful to predict (buy/not-buy, click/not-click, churn/not-churn, and stay/quit, for example).

Imagine I give you a set of images of cats and dogs (input). For each image, I also tell you whether this is a cat or a dog (label or

---

[10] Check www.python.org and www.r-project.org.

output). The ML algorithm can be trained in these images to create a classification model. This is illustrated in Figure 26.

Figure 26: The Machine Learning (ML) algorithm trains a model to separate images of cats and dogs.

Now, I can give a new image, and if you inject it into the model, it will provide you with the probability of being a cat and a dog (the highest wins). This process is shown in Figure 27.

Figure 27: The Machine Learning (ML) model can now classify new images into either cat or dog.

This is an example of supervised learning. We will discuss supervised and unsupervised learning further in the next section.

Machine learning approaches

Knowing what supervised and unsupervised learning are will help you communicate effectively with data scientists and machine learning engineers. There are three main types of machine learning approaches:

- **Supervised learning**: The algorithm is trained on labeled data, meaning each input is associated with a known output. It is used in classification, predicting a class (for example, spam or not spam), and regression (predicting a numerical value like temperature). More on classification and regression later in this chapter.

- **Unsupervised learning**: The algorithm works with data that has no predefined labels. It identifies patterns and structures such as clustering (for example, customer segmentation) and anomaly detection (like fraud detection). Unlike supervised learning, which relies on known labels to guide learning, unsupervised methods must identify trends and groupings directly from the input data alone. Among the most well-known tasks in unsupervised learning are clustering, dimensionality reduction, and outlier detection.

- **Reinforcement learning**: The algorithm involves allowing the system to interact with the environment and receiving rewards (or penalties) based on its actions. While the field is promising, it is not yet widely used in business. The main reason is that such systems require a large number of interactions with the environment to learn. This is often not practically feasible in a business setting. For more information, I suggest the book "The Hundred-Page Machine Learning Book" by Andriy Burkov.

Unsupervised learning

Unsupervised learning refers to a class of machine learning techniques where the algorithm receives no explicit feedback or labeled output during training. Instead, it explores the underlying structure of the data to discover hidden patterns. Let's detail the most common one: clustering.

Clustering

As a decision maker, be aware of the concept of clustering. This can provide ideas on how to use such approaches in your business, for example, for customer segmentation. Clustering is a process that partitions a dataset into distinct groups or clusters based on similarity (see Figure 28). These clusters are formed according to a predefined distance metric and are expected to be both compact (with points close to each other) and well separated (distinct from other clusters). In practice, clustering serves to assign pseudo-labels to unlabeled datasets, facilitating further analysis.

Clustering has broad applicability. It is used in customer segmentation, web search result grouping, and gene expression analysis, among others. For instance, at a retail company, clustering techniques help segment customers based on purchasing behaviors, enabling targeted marketing.

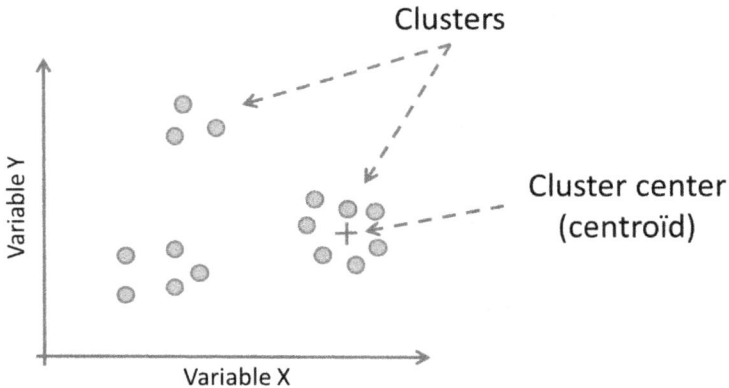

Figure 28: Examples of clusters in a dataset with two variables (columns).

A variety of clustering algorithms are available; each is suited to different types of data. These include:

- **Partitional clustering** (for example, K-means), which divides data into a predefined number of non-overlapping subsets.
- **Hierarchical clustering** (for example, BIRCH), which builds a hierarchy of clusters.
- **Density-based clustering** (for example, DBSCAN), which identifies clusters of arbitrary shape.
- **Grid-based clustering** (for example, STING), which uses a grid structure to summarize the data space.

K-means remains one of the most popular methods due to its simplicity and efficiency. The algorithm starts with an arbitrary selection of K centroids, assigns data points to the nearest centroids, recalculates the centroids based on these assignments, and repeats this process until the centroids stabilize. However, K-means has its limits: it struggles with non-spherical clusters, varying cluster densities, and outliers.

One key question in clustering is determining the right number of clusters in the dataset using data-driven (based on validity indices[11]) or business-driven (having an expert fix a number) approaches. Despite its technical rigor, clustering is inherently subjective. The results depend not only on the algorithm and data but also on how one defines a meaningful cluster. As noted in "Data Clustering: a Review":

Clustering is a subjective process [...] This subjectivity makes the process of clustering difficult.

Ultimately, the success of a clustering application is measured not by statistical metrics alone, but by its relevance and value to the business context. Because of the above-mentioned points, clustering is not as widely used as supervised learning approaches within companies.

A common use of clustering is to group your customers into similar categories. You first run a clustering algorithm (such as K-

---

[11] For more information, you can read the article "A bounded index for cluster validity".

means) on your customer data. Then, you investigate each cluster independently by looking at the average population. For example, you may discover that one group is composed of frequent, but low-value, customers. Another group may be very active on your website, and so on. Based on that, you can decide to adapt your marketing content and channels for each of these clusters.

Supervised learning

Since most machine learning deployed within companies is based on supervised learning, knowing what this is helps you understand what is needed to build these systems. Supervised learning is a fundamental type of machine learning where the algorithm learns from labeled data. Each training example consists of inputs and a corresponding output, also known as the label. The objective is to learn a mapping from inputs to the output that can generalize well to new, unseen data. This contrasts with unsupervised learning, where the goal is to uncover hidden patterns in data without predefined labels.

This learning approach underpins a wide range of practical applications, including predicting the next product a customer might buy, preventing customer churn, forecasting sales, and detecting objects in images. A common trait of supervised learning projects is that the minimum amount of labeled data required is not known in advance. We often proceed by trial and error, testing how the algorithm performs as more data becomes available.

Several well-established algorithms fall under the category of supervised learning. These include logistic regression, decision trees, random forests, support vector machines, and neural networks. Each algorithm has its strengths and drawbacks.

One thing to keep in mind when using supervised learning is only to use authorized input data. If the data you use as input (the variables or columns) isn't available in production, because it is unknown, this may be due to data leakage. As explained in "Becoming a Data Head":

Data leakage happens when a concurrent output variable masquerades as an input variable.

Cases of data leakage may be quite subtle. For example, I worked on a stock prediction tool in the past. To validate it, we did back-tests (testing the system back in time). The data leakage we introduced was to select companies that were active both at the beginning and the end of the back-test period. This is "cheating" in a way, since in reality, you cannot focus only on these companies.

Decision trees

Let's review a decision tree, which is both common in machine learning applications and easy to visualize and interpret once created. As a decision maker, you will love decision trees. They offer a way to dig into predictions and understand how each decision is made within the model. Decision trees are indeed particularly popular due to their simplicity and interpretability. They work by recursively splitting the dataset into subsets based on the value of input attributes. Let's take an example with the Iris dataset, which we presented before in the book. As a reminder, the iris dataset is composed of 150 measurements of 4 variables (input) on three categories of flowers (output). See Figure 29 to visualize both input and output.

Input   Output

Sepal length	Sepal width	Petal length	Petal width	Class
5.1	3.5	1.4	0.2	Iris-setosa
4.9	3.0	1.4	0.2	Iris-setosa
4.7	3.2	1.3	0.2	Iris-setosa
4.6	3.1	1.5	0.2	Iris-setosa
5.0	3.6	1.4	0.2	Iris-setosa
5.4	3.9	1.7	0.4	Iris-setosa
4.6	3.4	1.4	0.3	Iris-setosa
5.0	3.4	1.5	0.2	Iris-setosa
4.4	2.9	1.4	0.2	Iris-setosa
4.9	3.1	1.5	0.1	Iris-setosa
5.4	3.7	1.5	0.2	Iris-setosa
4.8	3.4	1.6	0.2	Iris-setosa
4.8	3.0	1.4	0.1	Iris-setosa
4.3	3.0	1.1	0.1	Iris-setosa
5.8	4.0	1.2	0.2	Iris-setosa
5.7	4.4	1.5	0.4	Iris-setosa

Figure 29: Sample of the Iris dataset with indications of input and output for supervised learning.

In the present case, we show data in row (samples) and column (features) format. This is the most common method for storing data in machine learning projects. One exception is the case of forecasting.

In the case of forecasting, we have an explicit notion of time and therefore data is displayed as a time series (simply a list of time-sorted values). We will discuss forecasting in more detail in Chapter 6. For more information, I also advise the book "Demand Forecasting for Managers".

Let's come back to the row and column format. The decision tree algorithm splits the space to separate the three classes as quickly as possible, aiming to create the smallest tree. Each internal node represents a decision on a variable, and each leaf node corresponds to a final classification. For example, the algorithm may start by checking whether the petal length is less than 2.5 cm to decide if a sample belongs to the Setosa species (see Figure 30).

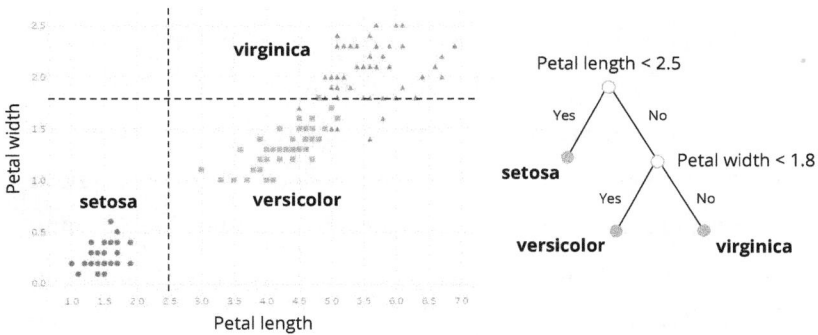

Figure 30: Example of a decision tree built on the Iris dataset. On the left, we show the split visually. On the right is the corresponding decision tree.

Many variations of decision tree algorithms exist (such as ID3, C4.5, and CART). More advanced methods, like Random Forests and Gradient Boosted Trees, combine multiple trees to improve accuracy and robustness. These ensemble learning approaches reduce the risk of overfitting and improve generalization on complex datasets (see Chapter 6).

Decision trees offer several advantages. They are easy to interpret, support both categorical and numerical data, perform implicit feature selection, and can handle missing values. Also, as noted in "Introduction to Data Mining":

> *Decision tree algorithms are quite robust*
> *to the presence of noise.*

However, they have limitations. They struggle with complex decision boundaries that involve combinations of features and may perform poorly when dealing with many target classes.

In summary, supervised learning remains a cornerstone of AI systems, especially when historical data with known outcomes is available. Its effectiveness lies in its ability to model relationships between inputs and outputs, making it a powerful tool for decision support and automation in businesses. So, machine learning models are very powerful. But keep in mind that, as noted in "Future Ready":

> *It [models] only makes predictions based on 'what it*
> *knows' about the world, which will never be complete.*

Once the ML algorithm has been chosen, we still need to set some parameters to make it work properly: this is called parameter fine-tuning. In the case of a decision tree, this would be deciding the maximum depth of the tree or when to stop splitting the tree further. In the case of neural networks, this would be deciding the number of layers and the number of neurons per layer. While data scientists can spend quite a lot of time on this task, existing ML tools and platforms have a high level of automation to fine-tune your model properly. So, do not spend too much time on this part of the process (see more details in Chapter 8).

Other algorithms

A decision maker needs to be aware of the various tools at their disposal to solve a given challenge. In addition to decision trees, several other families of algorithms exist, including logistic regression, support vector machines (SVMs), and neural networks. In the case of neural networks with multiple hidden layers, the approach is known as deep learning. However, on numerical data, forest-type approaches (for example, random forest and gradient boosted trees) have been proven to work exceptionally well.

In the continuation of the chapter, we will focus on the case of supervised learning, which is predominantly used in business. In my opinion, it is also where the real value for companies lies.

Building a machine learning model

Knowing how a machine learning model is built is key. Not only does it provide a view of what data scientists are doing. It also shows that there is no magic behind AI. We are "simply" running machine learning algorithms on top of, hopefully clean, data. When the business problem is clearly defined and the data is ready,[12] building[13] a machine learning model is done as follows:

1. **Split the data**: Divide data into two sets: a training set used to build the model, and a test set used to evaluate it.

2. **Build a model**: An ML algorithm identifies trends in the training data and builds a predictive model.

3. **Make predictions**: The newly built model is used to make predictions on the test set.

4. **Evaluate performance**: Accuracy is measured by comparing predictions with actual outcomes in the test set.

These steps are illustrated in Figure 31.

---

[12] We will discuss more about business understanding and data preparation in Chapter 8.

[13] In this book, we use the terms "building" and "training" a machine learning model interchangeably, with the same meaning.

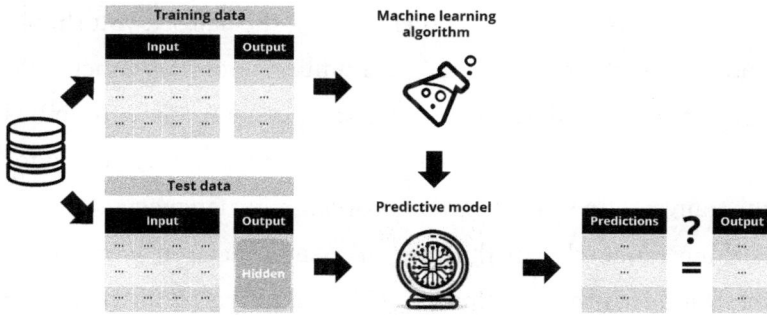

Figure 31: Schema representing how we build a machine learning model. First, the data is split into train and test sets. The model is built using training data. Test data is then thrown into the model to get predictions. These predictions are compared to the real output.

The main reason to split the data into a train and test set is to be able to test our model on "unseen" data (the test data that has not been used to train the model). On one side, we would like to keep the maximum data to train the model (usually, more data means a better model). On the other hand, we want to keep enough data for the test set to ensure our evaluation of accuracy is representative of future situations (when the model is in production).

When your dataset is too small to be split into a train and test set, you may want to turn to cross-validation. The concept is the same as with the train/test set but applied several times on randomly sorted data. With this approach, all of the dataset is leveraged and the final accuracy estimation is an average of each trial. While more time-consuming, this approach is definitely more robust. For more information, you can refer to the book "Data Science for Business".

Even if you may not be the one splitting the dataset, you should know that there is no magic number, and the exact split percentage depends on your use case. A general rule of thumb is to start with a split of 80/20 or 70/30 (the biggest value being for the train set). In most tools and programming languages, the split is done randomly. In the case of a small dataset, it might be interesting to use the option "stratified sampling". This will ensure that the distribution of your target variable is the same in the train and test sets (for example, the same proportion of cats and dogs images). For more information about stratified sampling, read the book "Applied Predictive Analytics" by Dean Abbott.

Classification and regression

As you may be the one defining the ML project, it is vital for you to understand the two main types of problems to solve, based on the variable you want to predict. Machine learning models typically solve two kinds of problems:

- **Classification**: When the outcome is a category, such as predicting if a customer will click on an ad or buy a product.
- **Regression**: When the outcome is a continuous value, such as forecasting sales or temperature.

Figure 32 shows a schematic representation of the classification and regression tasks.

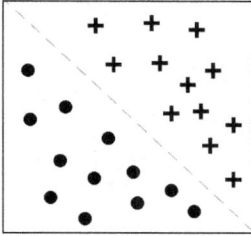

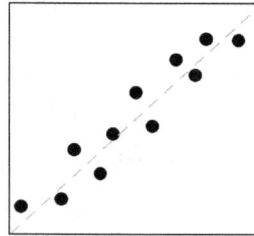

Classification

The output is a **category**
(click, buy, etc.)

Regression

The output is **continuous**
(sales, temperature, etc.)

Figure 32: Illustration of classification and regression in machine learning.

Understanding this distinction helps in selecting the appropriate algorithm and evaluation method. Classification tasks are easier to solve because we predict a class and not a precise number (fewer choices, thus easier for the algorithm). Also, measuring accuracy on a classification task is easier (see the next section). Therefore, in the case of a regression task, ask yourself: do I really need to solve it as a regression problem, or can I transform it into a classification one? For example, if predicting the pollen concentration for the next few days, do you need the exact value or would categories be enough (low, medium, high)?

Measuring model accuracy

As you will read reports and access presentations with machine learning metrics, you need to know what they mean. In a classification problem (with two classes), there is often one class that is more important from a business point of view (the clickers, the buyers). You will label this class as the "positive" one. To ensure a model performs well, it is essential to assess how accurate its predictions are. This can be measured in several ways:

- **Overall accuracy**: The proportion of all correct predictions over total predictions.
- **Precision**: Of the items predicted as positive, how many were actually positive?
- **Recall**: Of the positive items, how many did the model identify?

When evaluating results, the model makes two types of errors: false positives (predicted as positive when in reality it is negative) and false negatives (predicted as negative when in reality it is positive). This is shown using the so-called confusion matrix (see Figure 33).

Prediction

		Positive	Negative
Reality	Positive	True Positive (TP)	False Negative (FN)
	Negative	False Positive (FP)	True Negative (TN)

① Accuracy $= \frac{TP+TN}{TP+TN+FP+FN}$ ② Precision $= \frac{TP}{TP+FP}$ ③ Recall $= \frac{TP}{TP+FN}$

How many retrieved items are relevant ?   *How many relevant items are retrieved ?*

Figure 33: The confusion matrix, showing the two types of errors made in a binary classification project: False Positive and False Negative. Below are three metrics to evaluate the performance of a model.

Again, keep in mind that machine learning models are based on probabilities. Therefore, do not expect perfect models with 100% accuracy; this doesn't exist. In fact, as noted in "Future Ready":

Get suspicious if there is no error!

Once you have a machine learning system in production, it is quite easy to benchmark a new solution: it needs to be better in some way (more accurate, faster, etc.). But what about the first deployment? How do you evaluate the improvement of your data-driven approach?

Although there are several ways, one common approach is to find a naïve benchmark. For example, a simple average of similar cases. In the case of time series approaches, using the last day or month as the predicted value often provides a good benchmark. Indeed, if your ML models are not better than that, you should not use them.

This aspect is often overlooked in AI projects. Data scientists usually use complex, deep learning models without benchmarking them against simpler approaches or naïve benchmarks. This step is crucial to show the impact of the models you want to put into production. Indeed, you should always aim for the most straightforward and easiest to understand model first.

An example with pollen concentration

In the past, I worked on a project to predict pollen concentration in the coming days. We approached it as a time series problem. Our benchmark to beat was the pollen value on the current day. Indeed, the pollen concentration in the air is usually relatively stable; therefore, the value of today is already a good prediction for tomorrow.

The challenge of overfitting

You may ask yourself: why not always take the most complex model, so that we can capture all the patterns in the data? This is a valid question, and leads to the topic of overfitting. Overfitting is when a model learns the training data too well, including the noise, and fails to generalize to new data. These issues arise when we frequently use complex algorithms, while lacking sufficient data.

Avoiding overfitting requires striking a balance between model complexity and the ability to perform well on unseen data. Techniques such as train/test split and cross-validation, are used to address this issue. The difference between underfitting and overfitting is illustrated in Figure 34.

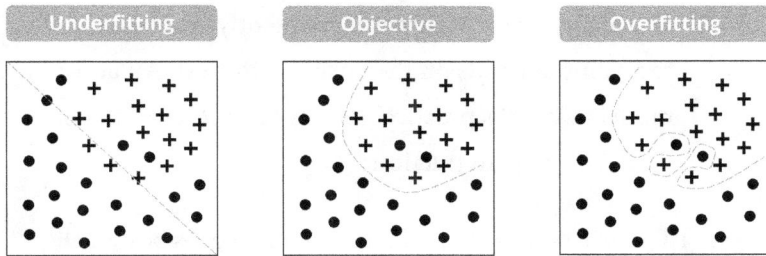

Figure 34: Illustration of the challenge of training the model correctly: underfitting and overfitting.

Keep in mind that what we want to achieve with machine learning is detecting and extracting trends or patterns from the data, while avoiding the noise.

Five things to keep in mind

Machine learning projects often face challenges that stem not from algorithms, but from foundational issues. Here are five key things to keep in mind while working on machine learning:

1. The quality of input data remains the cornerstone of any successful initiative. Poor data leads to poor outcomes, regardless of the algorithm used.

2. Data preparation typically consumes most of a data scientist's time, as ensuring clean, good quality, and well-structured data is essential before modeling can begin.

3. While algorithm accuracy is frequently emphasized, its real value depends on the business context. An accurate model that lacks practical relevance or interpretability often fails to gain traction.

4. There is no universal algorithm that works best in all cases; each domain and problem requires tailored methods.

5. Overfitting, where a model performs well on historical data but poorly in real-world scenarios, remains one of the most common and dangerous pitfalls. Train and test splits, as well as cross-validation, are methods to mitigate overfitting.

As noted above, there is no one-size-fits-all algorithm. While deep learning approaches work well on textual data and images, decision tree approaches are state-of-the-art for numerical data. The expertise and skills of the data scientist make the difference in how to approach a given problem, what to try, and what to do when results are not acceptable.

In a nutshell

This chapter provided an overview of the main concepts and families of machine learning models, with a focus on their practical use in business.

- **Clustering is one example of unsupervised learning**: In customer segmentation, for example, clustering techniques such as K-means help identify distinct groups that guide targeted marketing actions.

- **Decision trees are one example of supervised learning**: Decision trees are an interesting way to approach a classification problem because the model is interpretable, they can work with both categorical and numerical variables, and they can handle missing values.

- **Overfitting is a key challenge**: Making sure your model is fitting the trends in the data, and not learning the data by heart, is a key challenge in machine learning.

Machine learning is not just about algorithms but also about how well you frame the problem and prepare your data. In the next chapter, we present examples of AI applications. We cover different industries to open your mind to a broad horizon of possibilities.

Do you want to know more?

If you want to dive deeper into the field of machine learning, I can recommend the following books: "Predictive Analytics", "*Data Science for Business*", and "*Data Mining – Practical Machine Learning Tools and Techniques*".

Six

AI in Practice

AI is now used across many industries to solve business challenges. This chapter presents practical examples of how AI and machine learning can improve business outcomes—from sales forecasting and customer targeting to maintenance planning. We focus on the context, business challenges, and impact on the company. The examples show that while AI can bring substantial value, success depends on how well it is integrated into day-to-day operations.

Data-driven sales forecasting

Sales forecasting is a central activity in many companies. As a decision maker, you are likely to be confronted with forecasting at some point in your career. Forecasting enables the anticipation of customer demand, aligns internal operations, and facilitates better decision-making across departments. This example is about data-driven sales forecasting for a coffee company. Traditionally, sales forecasts relied on expert knowledge. However, with the availability of historical data and modern analytical tools, data-driven approaches have become both possible and desirable.

To set the right expectations, let's keep in mind the following points:

Forecasts are always wrong

This happens because of the following reasons:

- We assume that the future will behave like the past (which is not a perfect hypothesis).

- We represent reality with machine learning models. These models are an approximation of the real world. In fact, most information is not encoded into these models.

- We cannot predict rare events (war, COVID, etc.).

Even if the model provided perfect accuracy, forecasts will be incorrect for another reason. Think about why we make forecasts. We want to forecast the future to make informed decisions. As written in "Future Ready":

> [...] in reality we only want to know the future in order to be able to do something about it.

When we make these decisions, we change the future, and the original forecasts will become incorrect. So, forecasts are always wrong. However, they are still useful in helping us change the course of things and hopefully improve our business.

Forecasting adds value to the business only if internal stakeholders adopt it. The typical challenges in forecasting in a company setting are usually related to humans, not technology. As noted in "The Business Forecasting Deal":

Better forecasts, by themselves, are of no inherent value if those forecasts are ignored by management or otherwise not used to improve organizational performance.

In non-data-driven companies, data and AI initiatives must be sold to senior management. In this project, we estimated the added value of the project to convince senior leaders to fund it. We found different dimensions, such as the ones in Figure 35.

Figure 35: Three different dimensions for which a data-driven forecasting would be beneficial.

From skepticism to unrealistic expectations

AI projects are sometimes received with skepticism. Typical sentences we can hear are "How could that possibly work?" or "It will be impossible to beat 25 years of experience". Once the project has shown its impact, we quickly shift to unrealistic expectations: "Just changing the data should take you only one week," or "If it works with that category of products, it should work with all of them".

In the present project, stakeholders were initially skeptical about the feasibility of forecasting coffee sales without knowing all the details of specific markets. Once validated, some people adopted unrealistic expectations. So, be ready to sell your project and manage expectations at the same time. Here is an illustrative example of sales data per month (Figure 36):

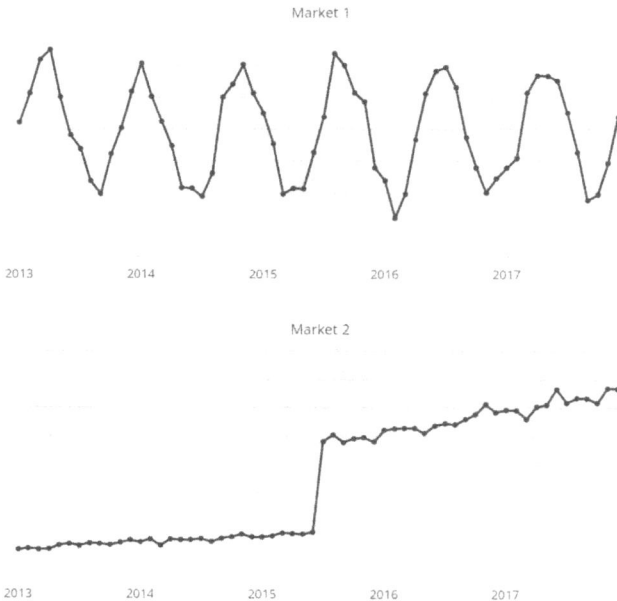

Figure 36: Illustrative time series data in two different markets.

What can you observe in the first plot? We see a clear seasonality (years "shape" are repeated). Obviously, predicting the following year will be an easy exercise. Now, looking at the second plot, the story is quite different. It would be much more complicated to predict the next months, as there is no clear pattern in the data.

Whatever algorithm you are using to do machine learning, whoever your data scientist is solving the problem, the performance of your model will be limited by the data itself (quantity, quality, and presence of patterns). Let's make a comparison with cooking: whatever cooking instruments you are using, whoever the chef is, the taste of your meal will be defined by the ingredients you have.

The coffee company has undergone a digital transformation. They launched a major initiative to generate accurate and standardized forecasts across global markets. This initiative was designed not only to automate forecasts but also to reduce bias and build trust between headquarters and local markets.

Forecasting is not just about predicting numbers, it is about ensuring the correct goods reach the right place at the right time. Low accuracy affects supply chain efficiency, customer satisfaction, and financial performance. In most companies, monthly forecast discussions take place between finance, sales, and supply chain (Figure 37).

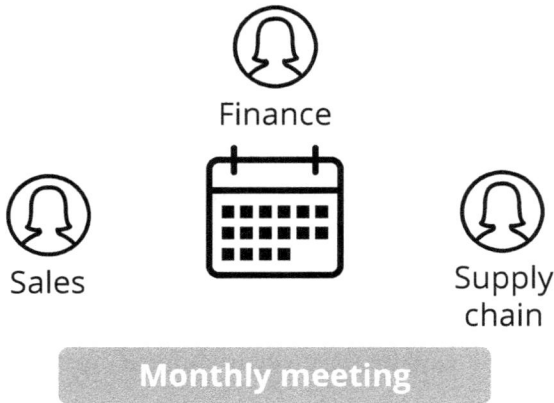

Figure 37: Review of past figures and agreement on future sales take place monthly between Sales, Finance, and Supply Chain. This process is sometimes referred to as S&OP (Sales and Operations Planning).

In our setting, we used a centralized approach. This means that we collect all data, produce and share forecasts for all products and markets. The project objective is to provide a data-driven forecast to demand planners in the supply chain department. Figure 38 shows the overall view of the system.

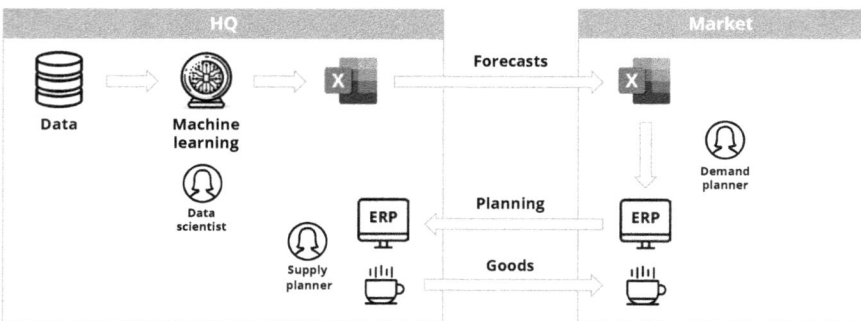

Figure 38: Representation of the forecasting process between headquarters and the markets.

Why Excel?

In this project, we used an advanced machine learning platform to produce the sales forecasts. Still, we shared these forecasts with the markets using Excel. Can you guess why? Often in AI projects, the tool can be a showstopper for the project. This means that people can refuse to adopt a solution because they need to learn a new tool. Sharing results in Excel ensures that no stakeholders will argue that they don't know how to use Excel. This is just one way to reduce the risk of stakeholders not adopting the project.

Forecasting models

While decision makers do not need to know all the details, understanding the main forecasting approaches helps them identify which data within the company can be leveraged for better decisions. Two types of forecasting models are used in this project:

- Univariate models, which only take historical data to make the predictions (such as exponential smoothing approaches).

- Multivariate models that use additional input factors (such as the ARIMAX algorithm).

Examples of additional input factors include promotions, number of boutiques, salesforce, and customer data (per month and market), as depicted in Figure 40. While more advanced and complex models are available, keep in mind that, as noted in "The Business Forecasting Deal":

> *Simple models will often forecast better than complex*
> *models, and simple processes may also be preferred.*

For more information on univariate and multivariate forecasting approaches, you can check the book "Forecasting, Principles and Practice".

Key questions in a forecasting project

These are key questions that you need to think about as a decision maker. You need to answer them during the project:

- What is the appropriate forecast horizon?
- What is the time aggregation (monthly, weekly)?
- What are the input variables to the algorithm (in addition to the sales history)?

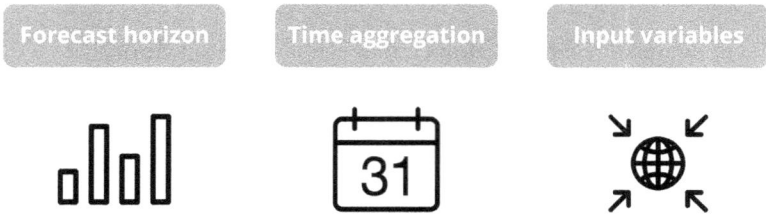

Figure 39: Three key questions to ask in any forecasting project.

An effective way to answer the last question is through brainstorming. Bring the different stakeholders together and discuss the potential variables to include. You can use the following impact versus feasibility matrix to separate the different input data and prioritize their collection (Figure 40).

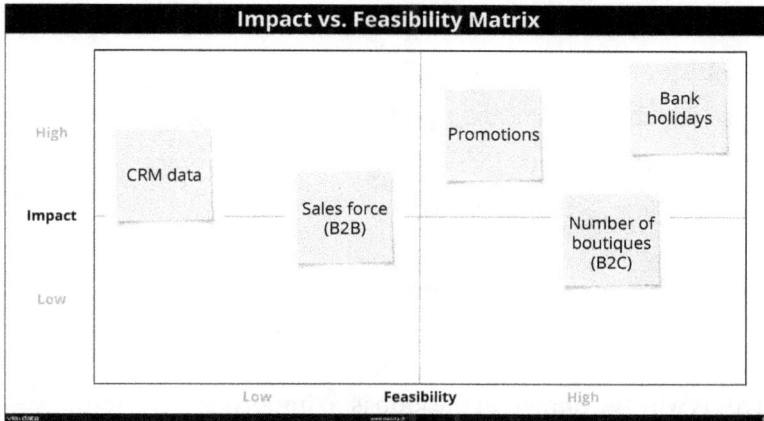

Figure 40: Displaying key input features for the sales forecasting project with the impact versus feasibility matrix. Impact is the expected importance of the feature, while feasibility is the expected ease of accessing it.

Impact and challenges

Understanding the impact and limitations of such a project is crucial for leading and integrating these initiatives within the company. In this project, we measured the impact, including improvements in forecast accuracy and the automation of manual tasks, across 40 markets. Despite automation, tools have a limited understanding of the business. For example, a model suggesting a flat forecast every month might minimize error statistically, but would not necessarily be trusted by stakeholders.

Thus, keeping the human in the loop is essential. Demand planners validate, adjust, and communicate forecasts. Their domain knowledge adds value beyond what any model can capture.

Trust is important in any AI project. In this one, it literally took months to build trust with stakeholders. With monthly forecasts, it is like sharing one data point per month. But, if you share nonsensical forecasts, let's say billions or flat forecasts, you kill trust in a few seconds. And as noted in "Fooled by Randomness":

Things are always obvious after the fact.

This is why the human in the loop is so important in AI initiatives.

Hotel revenue prediction

This project is interesting for decision makers as it provides a specific example of how AI can be leveraged to support sales in the company. In the online travel industry, understanding the value of potential hotel partners is critical. At a major online travel agency (OTA), where the business model is primarily commission-driven, predicting hotel revenue before onboarding is a strategic priority. The aim is to help sales teams prioritize high-revenue leads, enabling more effective acquisition and portfolio management.

Problem context

Before adding a hotel to its platform, the company must estimate the potential revenue that the property could generate. With millions of potential listings sourced from external websites, the scale and complexity of this task are significant. The challenge lies not only in predicting revenue accurately but also in identifying and managing duplicate hotel entries across various data sources. The schema of the project is depicted in Figure 41.

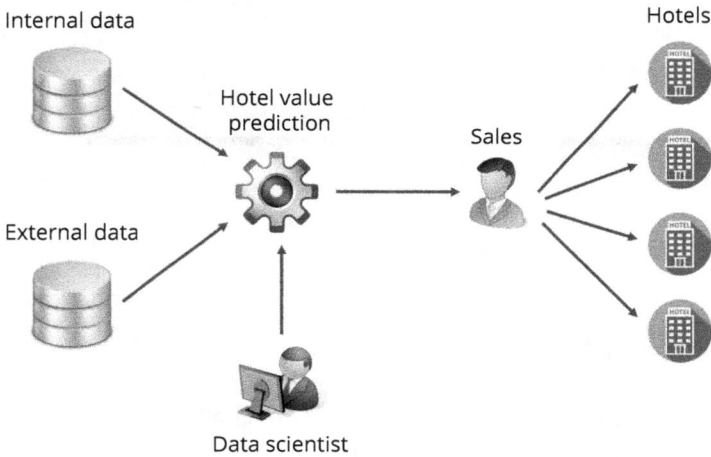

Figure 41: Hotel value prediction system in an online travel agency.

Data and features

To build the predictive model, various types of data were considered, ranging from location (region) to the number of rooms. We assessed these features based on their impact on prediction accuracy and the feasibility of their use, plotting them on an impact-feasibility matrix. This collaborative exercise helped identify high-priority features for model development (see Figure 42).

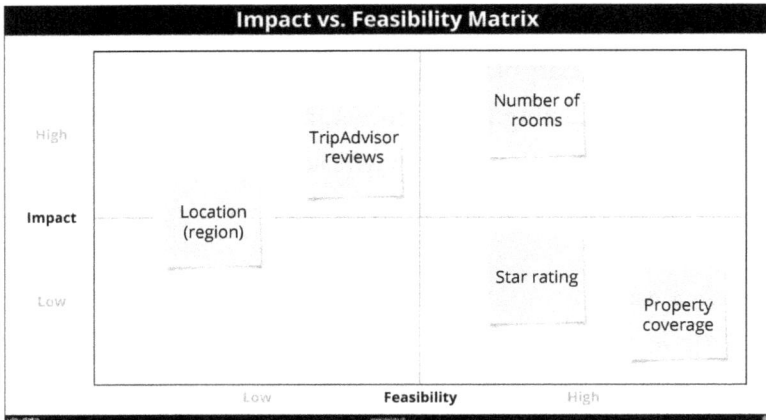

Figure 42: Displaying key input features for the hotel revenue prediction project with the impact versus feasibility matrix.

Modeling approach

To solve the hotel revenue prediction challenge, we adopted ensemble learning, primarily using decision trees as the base models. Knowing how ensemble learning works will help you, as a decision maker, better understand how far we can go with machine learning. In ensemble learning, different machine learning models are trained, for example, on a sample of the full dataset. Their results are then averaged. Figure 43 shows the concept of ensemble approaches within machine learning.

Ensemble methods, such as stochastic gradient boosted trees, combine the predictions of multiple models to deliver more accurate and robust results than a single complex algorithm. This approach draws inspiration from the *"wisdom of crowds"*, where collective predictions outperform individual insights.[14]

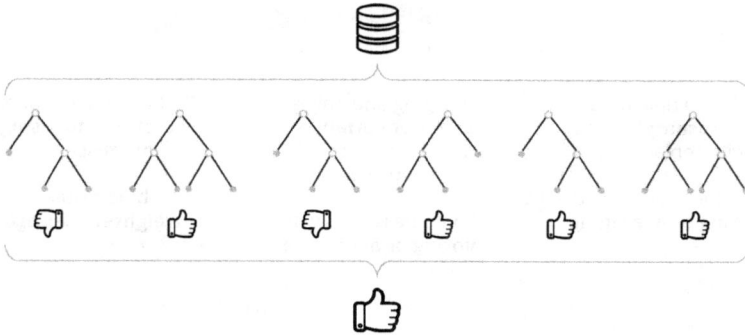

Figure 43: Illustration of the concept of ensemble learning in ML. Different machine learning models are trained and their results are averaged.

Three common approaches to ensemble learning are:

- **Bagging**: Building multiple models from resampled data (with replacement). This is the most basic form of ensemble learning.

- **Random forests**: Bagging and only a subset of variables is considered at each node split. This is the most common approach to ensemble learning.

- **Boosting**: Building multiple models iteratively, focusing on mistakes. This approach differs from bagging and random forests in that it is iterative.

---

[14] For more information, you can read *"The Wisdom of Crowd"* by James Surowiecki.

In Figure 44, these three approaches to ensemble learning are presented.

Bagging	Random Forests	Boosting
Build multiple models from **resampled data** (with replacement)	Bagging and only a **subset of variables** is considered at each node split	Build multiple models iteratively, **focusing on mistakes**
Combine results with **voting** or **averaging**	Combine results with **voting** or **averaging**	Combine results with **weighted average**

Figure 44: Three approaches to ensemble learning: bagging, random forests and boosting.

In this case, we illustrate ensemble learning with decision trees as their base models. Other machine learning algorithms can be used as the base approach and even a mix of them. You can find more information about ensemble learning in the book "Ensemble Methods in Data Mining".

Measuring success

When you reach the end of the first version of a project, you will have to decide how to improve it. You therefore need to know which kind of enhancements are feasible for an existing AI project. In this project, prediction performance was not evaluated solely by accuracy metrics but by its business impact. High-value hotels, as identified by the model, were found to generate several times more revenue than average hotels. To improve the results further, there are two potential axes:

- **Algorithms**: Fine-tuning the current model and trying other algorithms. This is fast, and the return on investment is low.

- **Data**: Improving the data (more data, greater diversity, and better quality). This is slow, and the return on investment is high.

Figure 45 shows this visually. To reinforce the importance of data (over algorithms), Peter Norvig, Google Research Director, said:

We don't have better algorithms than anyone else. We just have more data.

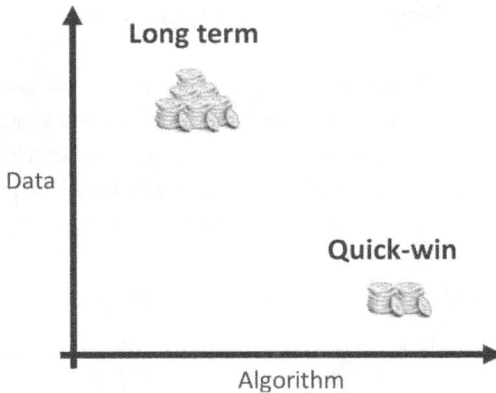

Figure 45: Two axes when trying to improve an existing AI project: algorithm and data.

Lessons learned

Several insights emerged from this project:

- Data quality is the primary factor affecting model performance. Efforts to improve input data yielded better results than algorithm changes.
- Trust in model predictions is influenced by variability. Reducing prediction variability helps build stakeholder confidence.
- Model training time can be significant and the choice of the algorithm must therefore be adapted to the business needs.

This case demonstrates how predictive modeling, combined with effective data strategies, can generate substantial value in the travel industry.

Deep dive on prediction variability

In machine learning, the variability of your predictions can kill your project. This means that if your predictions vary too much each time you share new figures, stakeholders will lose trust. In the case of this project, to avoid losing trust and adoption, we decided to set a limit on prediction variability. The prediction for a given hotel could not change more than a fixed percentage in one update of the model. This is frustrating from a data scientist's point of view (since better predictions are available), but it is of enormous value for the overall adoption of the project.

Online ads targeting

Here is an example that will show you how to link different datasets in your company to get a more comprehensive view of your customers. In this project on online ads targeting at a telco company, we used data and machine learning to deliver personalized digital experiences. Unlike traditional advertising, which reaches a broad audience, online targeting allows for one-to-one communication with users. This approach aims to increase engagement and improve conversion rates by presenting the right message to the right person at the right time.

Context

We can use several approaches for online targeting, each with examples of typical data:

- **Demographic targeting**: age, gender, income level
- **Contextual targeting**: page content or theme
- **Behavioral targeting**: user browsing history and actions
- **Geographical targeting**: user location via IP address
- **Temporal targeting**: time of day or day of the week.

In this project, we used a mix of CRM data (what we call "*customer data*") and website behavior (which we call "*web data*"). Here are examples of data sources:

- **Customer data**: Customer activity such as usage of services, purchase history, and interaction frequency.
- **Web data**: Pages viewed, time spent, number of visits, and clicks on ads.

Linking customer and web data is possible when the following conditions are met: the user visits the website of the company, and they are a customer of the telco company. Linking both worlds (customer and web) allows the creation of an extended customer profile (see Figure 46).

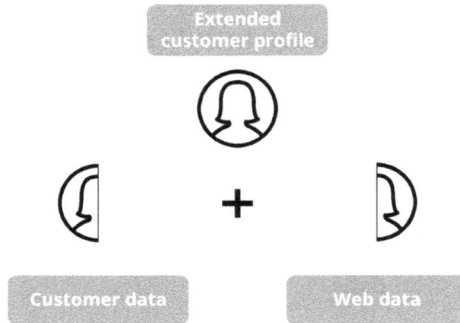

Figure 46: Linking the customer with web data allows the creation of an extended customer profile.

Examples of data used in this project are provided in Figure 47.

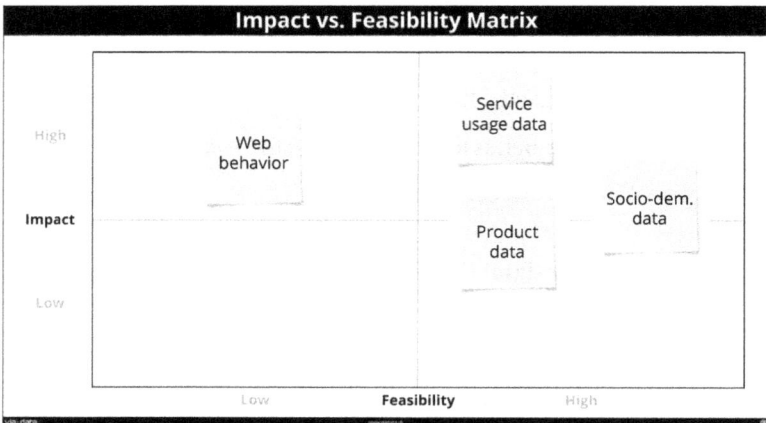

Figure 47: Displaying key input features for the online ads targeting project with the impact versus feasibility matrix.

Approach

Understanding the approach taken is important as it will help you appreciate how we can evaluate the performance of a machine learning model. Here are the steps we took to prepare the data and build the predictive model for this project:

1. Collect customer and web data for a specific period (for example, the last 30 days).
2. Build machine learning models (one model per ad) to predict which ad each customer is most likely to click on.
3. Score all visitors and segment them based on the predicted behavior.

To measure the effectiveness of the predictive model, we ran A/B tests with control groups (10% of users receive no personalization), as shown in Figure 48.

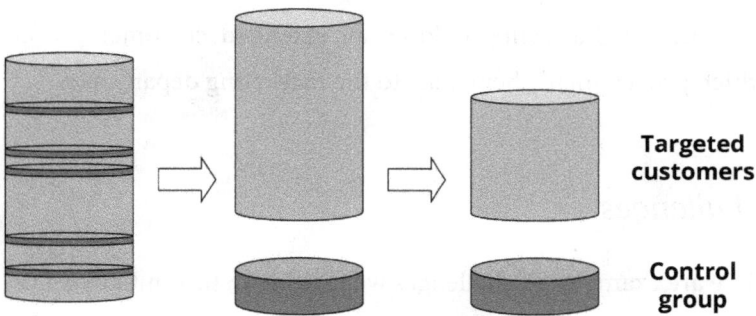

Targeted customers

Control group

Figure 48: A control group checks the effectiveness of the predictive model.

The use of control groups is typical as a way to test the business impact of a machine learning model. It is also commonly used in healthcare and medicine. A more advanced way to perform this test is the multi-armed bandit approach, which optimizes the notion of the control group. You can read more about it in the article "Introduction to Multi-Armed Bandits". Keep in mind that, as explained in 'The Value of Business Analytics":

> *[...] an improvement in the accuracy of a predictive model may be a positive outcome, but unless it changes something for the organization in a measurable way, it has not yet actually delivered any value.*

Impact

Here are examples of the impact we achieved in this project. First, we saw a significant improvement in click-through rates (CTR) for most targeted ads. Second, in the case of internal product ads, we measured a higher conversion rate. Ultimately, we gained valuable insights while building an extended customer profile, which proved highly beneficial to the marketing department.

Challenges

Here are examples of challenges we faced with this initiative:

- **Shared devices**: Models may incorrectly attribute behavior in multi-user households. Indeed, the targeting is performed at the household level, not individually.

- **Clicks needed**: The minimum number of required clicks was not achieved in all ad campaigns. Some were not interesting enough to generate sufficient data to build the model.

- **Operational delay**: Collecting enough clicks to build the first machine learning model for a given campaign can take up to two weeks.

Online targeting is a practical application of AI that illustrates how data can enhance customer interaction and business outcomes.

Exploring horizons

AI is no longer limited to large tech companies or academic labs. Today, it powers innovation across sectors, from healthcare to energy. This section presents real-world AI applications, exploring horizons to broaden your mind. Decision makers need to zoom out and get a good idea of what is feasible with AI.

The most common application

One of the most common uses of AI, or at least one of the first to become widely spread in companies, is to leverage CRM data for marketing purposes. Customer segmentation and cross-selling are typical examples. For more information, you can read "Data Mining Techniques in CRM".

Predicting length of stay

Hospitals aim to optimize bed occupancy and plan staff efficiently. AI models use patient demographics, medical history, and diagnostic data to predict how long each patient will stay. However, the value of these predictions depends on the quality of input data and the hospital staff's understanding of data-driven approaches. Building data literacy is crucial to adoption. This project showed a key point for any AI project: you need (quality) data. While the volume of data was there, we discovered that in most cases, the end user was not inputting data correctly, therefore preventing the use of AI to predict the length of stay. The only way to solve this problem is to train users on the importance of correct data collection.

Preventing payment defaults

Insurance providers seek to reduce defaults and the resulting legal costs. AI helps by identifying customers likely to miss payments, enabling timely reminders and proactive interventions. Still, fear and skepticism around AI often limit its use. Awareness campaigns and change management are needed. In this case, it took significant effort to motivate specific stakeholders to bypass their fear or low interest in AI to collaborate on the project.

Reducing patient churn

Patients using electronic auto-injectors sometimes discontinue treatment. AI identifies behavioral and contextual factors that predict churn risk, allowing for early interventions. Yet, prediction is not enough; reports and dashboards must translate insights into actionable steps for clinicians and business teams. This case highlights the importance of sharing insights with stakeholders throughout the journey, rather than waiting for the final predictive model to be put into production. Remember, your stakeholders want insights, not models.

Grouping news by topic

Financial analysts must track trends quickly. AI algorithms process thousands of articles to cluster them by topic, creating a visual "semantic landscape" that improves communication and decision-making. Yet, the challenge lies in leveraging these visual tools effectively. Indeed, a nice visualization is one thing. Getting insights and decisions based on a visualization is another thing. It is therefore important to keep in mind that visuals and dashboards are nice tools, but we need to think about how end users will drive decisions with these tools.

Targeting renewable energy campaigns

Low engagement in renewable energy campaigns prompted a new approach. AI models analyzed past performance to identify regions with higher adoption potential. In contexts with few positive outcomes, companies must adjust target definitions to maintain model reliability. In this specific case, the number of final customers was not large enough to train a machine learning model. We decided to go one level up in the conversion funnel and focus on leads who were interested in the product. This way, we had enough data to predict not who would buy, but rather who was interested in the product.

Understanding perfume formula proximity

AI models reveal subtle relationships between ingredients in perfume formulas, improving attribute predictions and supporting product development. However, evaluating use cases in isolation may miss interdependencies; a holistic analysis is more effective. In this specific project, we could not show the generated value directly. Instead, this new way of thinking and processing data was the basis for many future AI projects, which generated revenue for the company. Therefore, try to keep in mind the value of your AI initiatives as a whole and not only individually.

Predicting machine output temperature

For machines processing pet food, AI predicts output temperature to optimize operations. This improves efficiency, but only if users trust and understand the model's outputs. In this project, we deployed the first AI model, which proved to increase performance but had no impact on production. We discovered that the technician working on the machine was not trusting the automatic mode and was continuously working manually. Therefore, any improvement in the machine's functioning, whether with or without AI, would have no impact. We rolled out a new version, showing the predicted output temperature to the technician in near real-time. As trust in the system increased, so did the impact on production.

Detecting security ink counterfeits

For important documents containing security ink, AI analyzes spectral ink signatures to detect fakes. It allows for the detection of genuine inks from fake ones. The detection is performed through hand-held devices used by the police and customs officers. The more variability you have in your data, the more robust your machine learning model will be. Indeed, the more examples your system has been exposed to, the better its generalization capacity will be. In the case of the security ink detection project, the first version of our model was primarily trained on data collected from right-handed individuals. Therefore, our system was initially not performing well with left-handed users.

Forecasting watch repairs

Repairing luxury watches requires planning for skilled labor. AI forecasts future repair volumes based on past sales and warranty claims, enabling proactive resource allocation. One key point to understand here is the challenge for watch manufacturers to find experienced talent to repair precision watches. Therefore, being able to forecast watch repairs helps the company allocate resources around the world. In this case, AI was used to challenge an existing human-based forecast. The data-driven approach is also a valuable complement for discussing and reviewing human output.

Predicting elevator failures

Lifts operate day and night and need regular maintenance to work properly. However, unexpected incidents may mean that the elevator is down for maintenance. In this case, a technician comes on-site to repair it. To avoid such cases, it is useful to predict elevator failures. In this supervised learning project, the main challenge was the low number of past failures to train a model. In this case, we ultimately utilized insights from the data to identify a proxy for failure and notify the company that the elevator was likely out of service.

A never-ending story

And there is much more. AI can be used to predict where to put the next telecommunication antenna, detect defective products in manufacturing, evaluate emotions in video games, optimize product prices in real-time, recommend the next customer purchase, personalize marketing campaigns, predict the whole customer journey, and the list goes on. As written in "Analytics – How to Win with Intelligence":

> *Indeed, these analytics systems seem limited only by the imagination.*

For these AI use cases to have an impact on the company, they need to work in production. Therefore, your company needs to have database systems, data pipelines, and tools to enable these AI systems to run in production. In the end, it is about getting AI integrated into existing (or new) processes within your company. You therefore need to be able to design systems in which AI can be integrated smoothly.

In a nutshell

This chapter presented three real-world applications of AI—sales forecasting, hotel revenue prediction, and online ads targeting—

as well as several examples of real AI projects to open your mind to what is feasible with AI.

- **Sales forecasting requires both trust and adoption**: In the coffee company example, forecasts were shared via Excel to ensure usage by local markets, and human validation was kept to avoid losing trust through unrealistic figures.
- **Hotel revenue prediction shows the power of feature selection**: Using an impact-feasibility matrix helped prioritize useful input data and improved model effectiveness in predicting hotel values.
- **Online targeting benefits from combining customer and web data**: By linking customer records with website behavior, the telco company created extended customer profiles and improved ad click-through and conversion rates.

These examples demonstrate that the value of AI depends on both the quality of the data and the effectiveness of the solution's integration into existing workflows. In the next chapter, we enter the world of Generative AI and chatbots. We explain the specificities of these approaches and provide tips for using them.

Do you want to know more?

If you are interested in the topics covered in this chapter, I can recommend the following books: *"Prediction Machines"*, *"Data Juice"*, and *"Business Forecasting"*.

SEVEN

Generative AI and Chatbots

Generative AI brings a new way for machines to create content, such as text, images, or videos. Unlike traditional models that describe or predict, these models produce new outputs by learning patterns from data. This chapter explains how generative models work, their applications, and their limits. It also discusses methods to improve results. Real-world examples demonstrate how companies can effectively apply these models, while also considering the importance of trust, human oversight, and ethical considerations.

Understanding Generative AI

Most of your colleagues are likely to use some Generative AI tools in their work. For this reason, decision makers need to understand what's happening under the hood. It will help you know what is feasible (or not) with such approaches.

Generative AI (GenAI) represents a new approach for machines to interact with data and generate new content. Unlike models focused on description or prediction, Generative AI is designed to produce text, images, videos, and other forms of content, based on what it has learned from existing data.

Generative AI works by learning the underlying structure and patterns of existing data. Once trained, it can generate new and original outputs that resemble the data it has studied. A simple way to think about it is that Generative AI does not memorize exact examples but rather learns how the examples are structured and builds new ones following the same principles.

In the example below (see Figure 49), we show the original idea behind Generative AI: predicting the next word.

The cat is lying on the

pillow	40%
couch	30%
bed	15%
carpet	10%
fridge	5%

Figure 49: Example showing how Generative AI works by predicting the next word in a sentence.

If the sentence (input) is "The cat is lying on the", then the prediction (output) might be "pillow". Note that, as always in machine learning, it is based on probabilities. Therefore, other words are possible as predicted outputs (couch, bed, etc.). Once the word is predicted, the new completed sentence is used as input to predict the most likely next word, and so on.

Large Language Models (LLM)

In the rest of the book, I will sometimes use the term Large Language Models (LLM). LLMs are models that have been pre-trained on a large amount of text (such as data from the internet and books). These pre-trained models serve as the foundation for chatbots like ChatGPT. In the case of Generative AI, you usually don't build the model yourself (see Chapter 8), but instead use existing LLMs and provide input (the so-called prompt). More information will be provided later in this chapter.

The GPT model

Since ChatGPT is the most common Generative AI tool nowadays, it is useful to know what is behind its name. Generative AI models like GPT (Generative Pre-trained Transformer) are built around three key ideas:

- **Generative**: They generate new content based on a given prompt.
- **Pre-trained**: They are trained on massive amounts of text data before being fine-tuned for specific tasks.

- **Transformer**: They use a Transformer[15] architecture to understand relationships between words.

The model's main task is to predict the next word in a sequence, an approach that enables it to produce coherent and meaningful text. In the picture below, we explain the hierarchy between the different Generative AI terms (Figure 50).

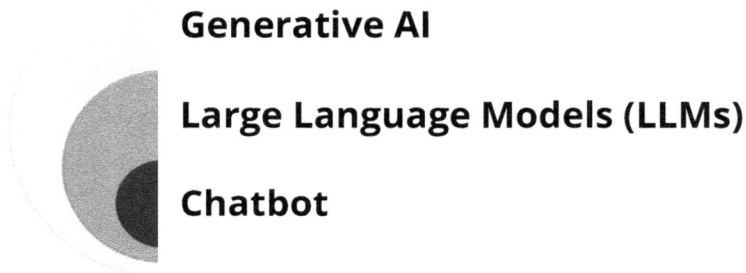

Generative AI

Large Language Models (LLMs)

Chatbot

Figure 50: The Generative AI terminology related to Large Language Models and chatbots.

The power of Large Language Models (LLMs) lies in their ability to be pre-trained automatically and solve multiple challenges. As explained in Denis Rothman's "Transformers for Natural Language Processing":

> *The model can then perform a wide range of tasks with no further fine-tuning.*

---

[15] Transformers are specific deep learning architectures that process data by focusing on the most important parts using a mechanism called attention.

We often hear about ChatGPT as a chatbot based on Generative AI. While this is the most well-known chatbot since the end of 2022, it is definitely not the first one. Eliza is often cited as one of the first convincing chatbots. Eliza is a Natural Language Processing program developed in the 1960s at MIT. It was primarily created to explore communications between humans and machines. Eliza already fooled people, as noted in "Rebooting AI":

> *Despite Eliza's paper-thin understanding of people, many users were fooled.*

However, keep in mind that there are many such chatbots, paid or available for free. Some of them are good for specific tasks, such as generating images. Examples of chatbots include Copilot, Gemini, and Claude. The most well-known open-source LLM is Llama, by Meta.

Applications of Generative AI

As decision makers, you may have to find ways to automate manual tasks, accelerate processes, and avoid redundant work. Therefore, you need to have examples of how Generative AI is used across various sectors. Here are the most popular ones (Figure 51):

- **Customer Service**: Handling open-ended client inquiries.

- **Marketing**: Creating content for advertising campaigns.

- **Software Development**: Assisting developers by generating code.

Customer service	Marketing	Software development
Handling open-ended questions from clients	**Creating content** for advertising campaigns	**Generating code** to assist developers

Figure 51: Three typical domains in which Generative AI is used.

Here are three more specific examples of Generative AI use cases: hospital discharge letters, course planning, and literature review.

The hospital discharge letter-writing process is a time-consuming task that keeps many doctor assistants busy. While such letters have to be manually checked before sending, Generative AI can support drafting the letter and including the patient's medical records, discharge summaries, and treatment history. This reduces the administrative burden, minimizes errors associated with manual transcription, and enables clinicians to focus on reviewing and validating the content rather than writing it from scratch. One of the main challenges is related to patient data privacy, which creates the need for an LLM hosted internally.

Companies providing courses such as fire extinguishing and first aid training need to prepare complex course planning. These plans need to take into account several constraints, such as the time window, course location, minimum number of participants, and availability of course instructors, for example. Generative AI reasoning capabilities can be leveraged to propose plans with specific constraints. One significant advantage is the possibility to update any specification and regenerate the plan on the fly. The challenge is to keep in mind common-sense information that the LLM may miss.

In the medical industry, reviewing literature from several academic research studies is an important task. It can help in identifying gaps in clinical research, analyzing the competition, and defining the clinical strategy. Generative AI can be used to list studies in specific fields, within a particular timeframe, and provide a summary or a detailed table with results. Research articles can be analyzed to find gaps and, therefore, specific positioning for a new product. The challenge in such applications is the veracity of the sources used, which a human must check.

When you think about a new Generative AI use case for your company, start with a project for which it is easy to show the return on investment (a quick-win), scale the solution (from a proof of concept to production), and bring stakeholders on board (people already accepting the idea of using AI).

One example is generating marketing content. You can easily measure the time taken by the team to create social media content and therefore the return on investment from automating part of this process. This will help you select Generative AI projects that bring value, can be pushed into production, and are accepted by end users.

Enhancing Generative AI

To make informed decisions, you must leverage your own data. Therefore, knowing how to provide helpful information to Generative AI is vital for decision makers. Generative AI, at its core, is very generic. I often say that it provides you with the average of the web. This is, of course, an exaggeration, but it highlights the fact that LLMs have been pre-trained on generic data, not specific to your company or use case.

In that sense, Generative AI is not a competitive advantage for you and your company. Everyone has access to Generative AI chatbots and LLMs. Therefore, you need to customize existing tools and models to your needs. There are several ways to personalize and improve the performance and reliability of Generative AI models:

- **Prompt engineering**: Crafting prompts carefully to get better answers. This is the most basic approach (Figure 52). We will provide more details later in this chapter.

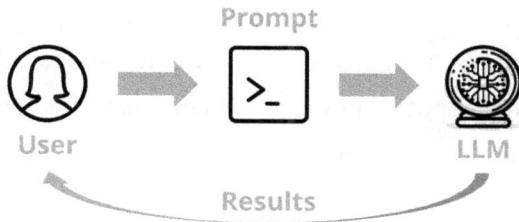

Figure 52: An illustration of the idea of iterating on your prompt to get the right results from an LLM.

- **Retrieval Augmented Generation (RAG)**: Leveraging existing (and internal) data to limit incorrect answers (Figure 53). This is done by checking for the right information in an internal database of your company, before answering your prompt. This allows for more specific and correct answers. However, this needs a specific setting within your company.

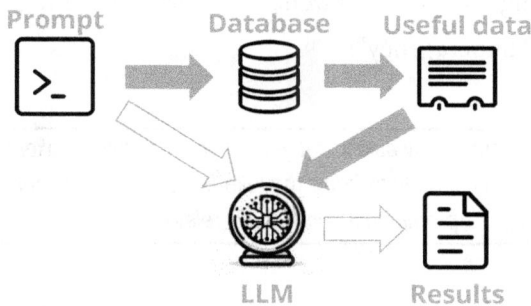

Figure 53: Illustration of the process of RAG (Retrieval Augmented Generation), allowing you to benefit from your company data while prompting an LLM.

- **Fine-tuning**: Training the model further on specific datasets to specialize it (Figure 54). Fine-tuning means updating an existing LLM to fit your company data, for example. This process is costly in terms of available data and computing power. It also means that you have senior data scientists available to perform this task.

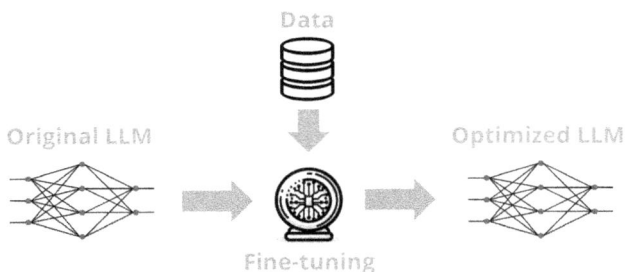

Figure 54: Illustration of the process of fine-tuning an existing LLM on specific data, such as your company data. This process is complex to perform.

Please keep one thing in mind: even though you may enhance Generative AI with advanced prompts, your own data, or fine-tune existing models, an LLM never "knows" anything. Instead, as written in "Superagency":

> *You are simply asking it [the LLM] to predict what tokens are most likely to follow the tokens that comprise your prompt in a contextually relevant way.*

The term hallucination is used to refer to answers from an LLM that seem correct but are not. People often encounter challenges with this and try to find ways to eliminate these errors. While the idea seems interesting, you have to keep in mind that Generative AI is based on probabilities. As noted in "Co-Intelligence":

> *The same feature that makes LLMs unreliable and dangerous for factual work also makes them useful.*

Similarly, in predictive approaches, we have seen examples of predicting ad clicks, future sales, and hotel revenue. In all these examples, the machine learning models always make mistakes since our models are not perfect. Therefore, if you want such Generative AI systems to be flexible, creative, and useful, you have to accept the errors they make. As noted in "Generative AI for Leaders":

> *In an age where AI can generate highly convincing text, the ability to critically evaluate information becomes more important than ever.*

Prompting

As a decision maker, you are likely to use Generative AI to be more efficient. Improving your prompts with a few tips will make you even more productive. The quality of a generative AI model's output heavily depends on the quality of the input it receives—this is known as prompting. A prompt is the instruction or question a user submits to the model. Writing effective prompts, also referred to as prompt engineering, is key to obtaining relevant, accurate, and useful responses.

Same prompt, different answers

Try the following exercise with your favorite chatbot: write a prompt and run it. Then rewrite the same prompt (several times if needed). What do you observe? Yes, the answer is sometimes different. This is normal since each word predicted has a certain probability of appearing; therefore, it may be replaced by another one. This replacement may also influence the next word and, therefore, the overall answer.

What makes a prompt effective?

An effective prompt clearly defines the task and includes sufficient context. A helpful framework for structuring prompts comprises three key elements, which I call the "3E":

- **Expertise**: Indicate the role the chatbot should take, such as a data analyst, marketing expert, or teacher.

- **Expectation**: State the expected outcome, including any constraints or specific requirements, such as the format or specific length.

- **Example**: Provide an example of the kind of output expected, such as a (non-sensitive) text you wrote or a summary style.

This structure helps the model better understand the intent behind the request and tailor its response accordingly. Also, remember to tell the LLMs to be critical if you want to be challenged. Indeed, they have been designed to please you, so do not expect to be contradicted by default.

You usually won't obtain the desired output with your first prompt. It is therefore key to work in iterations. Try with a first prompt, look at the result, and then iterate by modifying the prompt. If you have specific habits for all your prompts (such as using simple words or limiting the answer to five sentences), you can add these as custom instructions to the most common chatbots.

Tips for advanced prompting

To further improve the interaction with generative models, consider the following strategies (Figure 55):

- **Simplify complex queries**: Break down large or complicated requests into smaller, manageable parts.
- **Acknowledge uncertainty**: Ask the model to tell you when it is unsure or lacks sufficient information.
- **Request alternatives**: Ask for variations or different combinations to explore multiple perspectives.

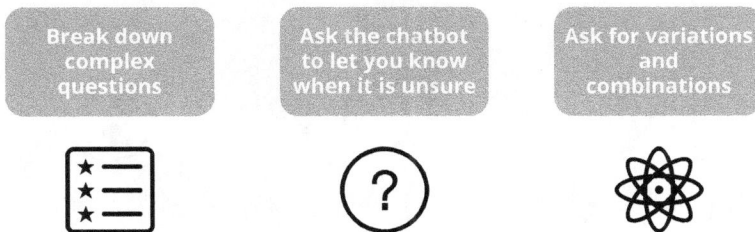

Figure 55: Advices for the advanced use of Generative AI.

Common pitfalls

As a leader, you need to show examples. Be aware of what not to do, and make sure your colleagues are informed. Even with well-written prompts, there are a few critical points to keep in mind (Figure 56):

- **Handle sensitive data carefully**: Never include personal or confidential information in prompts.

- **Verify results**: Always check the accuracy of the output. Generative models may produce content that seems plausible but is incorrect (what was referred to before as hallucinations).

- **Limit use**: Avoid overusing AI for tasks where it is not needed. The planet will be thankful to you. The topic of AI and the environment will be discussed in Chapter 9.

Figure 56: Three points to keep in mind when interacting with Generative AI.

There are different ways to measure the impact of AI, and particularly Generative AI, on the environment. It can be measured in water consumption used to cool data centers and tons of CO_2 emissions generated to train and operate LLMs. We provide further examples in Chapter 9.

Detecting AI content

At the time of writing this book, it is still very challenging (to say the least) to detect whether content, such as text or an image, has been AI-generated. OpenAI, the creator of ChatGPT, proposed a tool to detect AI-generated content. However, this tool was dismissed a few months later due to inaccurate results.

It is typically a challenge for schools to detect whether students have used Generative AI tools, and to what extent, to write essays. Note that this is not only a problem for us humans, but also for computers. Indeed, the power of Generative AI comes from the fact that it has learned from human-generated text and images. What about a future in which most of the text on the internet is machine-generated? How will it impact the performance of upcoming Generative AI systems?

The inability to reliably detect AI-generated content is a significant challenge for our society. Indeed, Generative AI tools are easy to access and use. Therefore, they open the door to abusive use of such tools to generate deep fakes and convey misleading information to a large audience. As explained in "Responsible Data Science":

A deepfake is an image, video, or audio track in which a real person is combined with synthesized elements of another imaginary or real person.

Imagine the impact a deep fake video of the US President could have if it were spread on social networks.

Patent and copyright issues

At the time of writing this book, copyright protection is not granted to works created using AI. As written in the Federal Register:[16]

This guidance explains that while AI-assisted inventions are not categorically unpatentable, the inventorship analysis should focus on human contributions, as patents function to incentivize and reward human ingenuity.

Note that this can evolve at any time in the future. What is important to keep in mind is that Generative AI should not be used to generate your final product image, brand, or logo, for example. However, you can use Generative AI to iterate during the process to develop marketing content and create the final piece with a human, in case you want to protect your creation.

---

[16] Source : www.federalregister.gov.

> **Is it learning from me?**
>
> You may wonder if chatbots are learning from you. If you think of the data that is about you available on the web (websites, blogs, etc.), then yes, the model certainly may have included this data in its training set. If you think about the current discussion you have with the chatbot, then no, it is not learning from those specific interactions. Some chatbots have memory settings and you can ask them to remember (or forget specific things you write).

Limits and challenges of Generative AI

You need to be aware that, like any tool, Generative AI has limits. It is key to realize that Large Language Models (LLMs) are indeed language models, not knowledge models.[17] This means they lack a common interpretation of the world that humans share. This is what is shown in Figure 57.

Language model　　　　**Knowledge model**

Figure 57: A language model does not mean a knowledge model. We should keep this in mind when using LLMs.

---

[17] Even though recent models are multimodal and can work with images and videos for example.

As noted in "Superagency":

> *As of yet, LLMs have no real capacity for commonsense reasoning, no lived experience, and no grounded model of the world.*

It is crucial to understand that Generative AI is not perfect:

- It tends to produce an average of the web, which is usually not very specific. As an example, it tells you how to make butter correctly, but it won't be able to design a specific strategy for your company to be successful.

- It may generate inaccurate or "hallucinated" information. If you ask it to write a positive comment about a festival you organized, which you never did, it will provide a comprehensive comment about the event.

- It lets you input sensitive data, which should not happen (like most systems). Do not input confidential data, company information, or valuable information in a chatbot. Always ask yourself the question: Would you put this information on your favorite social network?

Generative AI is different from predictive machine learning (as seen in Chapter 5). In Generative AI, the model is already trained. Therefore, you are using an existing AI. In the data science process, which we will cover in Chapter 8, the step "modeling" is not performed in the case of Generative AI.

Keep in mind that believing you are doing AI when using a Generative AI tool is like thinking you are Superman when you take a plane. Generative AI is a tool, and its proper use requires critical thinking. We will discuss more about the limits of Generative AI in Chapter 9.

While Generative AI has recently gone mainstream, we should remember that AI itself is not new. People have been using systems based on AI for decades. The books you see on Amazon, the movies suggested on Netflix, and the music you get recommended on Spotify, all of these are based on AI. So, what is so different about Generative AI and chatbots? It is about choices, as noted in "Superagency":

Finally, there was a highly accessible, easy-to-use AI tool that explicitly worked with you and for you, rather than on you.

In a nutshell

This chapter introduced the concept of Generative AI, with a focus on how it works, how to use it properly, and its limitations.

- **Generative AI is about creating new content**: These specific (large) models have been pre-trained on a massive amount of data, allowing them to cover a very wide range of (fuzzy) requests from users.

- **Hallucinations are part of the process**: Like predictive models, Generative AI will make errors. Accepting some level of inaccuracy is necessary to benefit from its flexibility and creativity.
- **LLMs are language models, not knowledge models**: They produce fluent text but lack a true understanding of the world, which can lead to misleading or nonsensical outputs.

Generative AI is a powerful tool, but getting results you can trust depends on how you use it and how well you understand its limits. In the next chapter, we explain the data science process and share best practices to select, prioritize, and execute data projects. We provide tips and tricks to increase the chances of success with your AI initiatives.

Do you want to know more?

In case you are curious about the topic of Generative AI, I can advise the following books: *"What is ChatGPT doing and why does it work?"*, *"Generative AI for Leaders"*, and *"Co-intelligence – Living and working with AI"*.

EIGHT

Best Practices in Data Science

Running a successful data science project takes more than choosing the right algorithm. It requires a clear method that connects business goals with data work. This chapter introduces a common framework to guide data projects through six key steps—from understanding the problem to deploying a solution. A real example shows how to apply this process in practice and highlights the importance of collaboration, communication, and trust. The chapter also discusses how to start a data project and how to prioritize use cases for maximum impact.

The data science process

Since you may be the one leading AI initiatives, you must understand the different steps of the data science process. You can see data science as a field that leverages data in a business context. The data science process below is standard in the sense that it is applicable across countries and industries.

Successfully delivering a data science project requires more than selecting an algorithm or improving model accuracy. A structured methodology is essential to ensure alignment with business goals, efficient execution, and long-term adoption. Among the recognized frameworks, CRISP-DM[18] (Cross Industry Standard Process for Data Mining) is the most widely used and offers a reliable approach through six key phases (Figure 58).

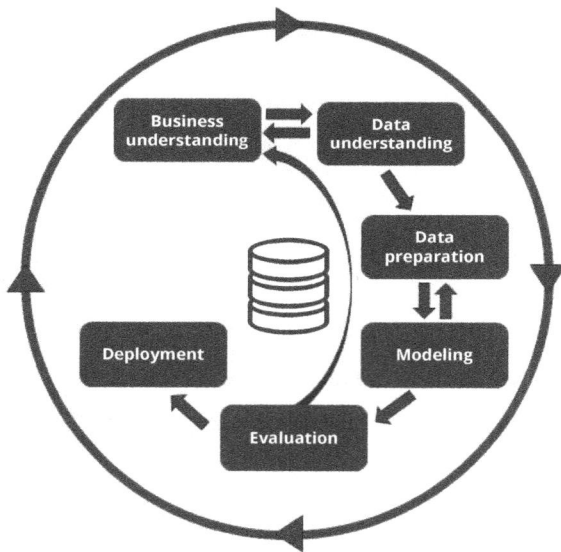

Figure 58: The CRISP-DM process for data science projects. It is composed of six main steps that you should perform for any data (science) project.

[18] Check the CRISP-DM document at www.tinyurl.com/the-crisp-link.

There are several other data science methodologies out there, such as the KDD Process (Knowledge Discovery in Databases) and SEMMA (Sample, Explore, Modify, Model, and Assess). We use the CRISP-DM framework in this book, as it is the most widely known and used.

In my experience, I have seen the CRISP-DM approach used for other data projects. For example, in the case of designing a dashboard, the process can be applied. The modeling phase would consist of creating the dashboard (instead of the machine learning model). I encourage you to use this approach for any data-related initiative you have in your company. This is also an excellent way to explicitly demonstrate that data and AI projects differ from standard IT developments.

1. Business understanding

The role of the decision maker is critical in this step. In one sentence, this phase involves transforming a business problem into a data or AI one. The project starts with a deep understanding of the business context. It is crucial to define the problem clearly and identify what success entails. For example, when predicting hotel value, one must determine whether accuracy or interpretability is more important for stakeholders. Domain experts must be included from the beginning to ensure that models address real-world constraints. As written in "Data Science for Business":

> *When faced with a business problem, you should be able to assess whether and how data can improve performance.*

In the examples shown in Chapter 6, one key question to ask in the business understanding phase is about the balance between accuracy and explainability of the project. Usually, very accurate models are more "black box" ones. On the other hand, we may want to have explainable models to build trust with stakeholders and explain our decisions. In the case of the hotel value prediction project, accuracy was selected as the most important. We return to explainable models in Chapter 9.

2. Data understanding

This phase focuses on exploring data sources. A common challenge is locating the right data (see Chapter 2) and understanding how it was collected and processed. Working closely with people who are familiar with the data is essential. This step includes both exploratory and explanatory data analysis. For example, in one project I worked on, customer age was imputed (to replace missing values). While this is the right solution in specific cases, some algorithms may work better with a missing value (rather than the imputed one, which also adds noise). Knowing that data was cleaned before you use it is important information.

Getting access to data is usually not the biggest challenge in companies. What I find more challenging is finding the person who collected the data. Indeed, you likely want to answer key questions such as why the data was collected, when, and with what processing. Hopefully, your company understands the importance of data and has already put in place data governance guidelines and, for example, deployed a data catalog.

3. Data Preparation

This phase is about making sure the data is right (see Chapter 2). Ask yourself the question: What can I do to help the computer with my domain knowledge? Raw data must be cleaned and transformed into a suitable format for modeling. This includes correcting data, handling missing values, removing or explaining outliers, and creating additional variables (columns). As with the previous steps, the presence of domain knowledge can guide the creation of relevant features and help explain anomalies in the data. This is a complex task, as noted in Dean Abbott's "Applied Predictive Analytics":

> *Each data set can provide different challenges to data preparation [...], rendering recipes for data preparation exceedingly difficult to create [...].*

While missing values and outliers might be quite easy to spot, finding and correcting wrong values is more challenging. Take time to consult with domain experts to define business rules to detect and update errors in your dataset.

There are two important points when processing outliers. First, defining what an outlier is depends on your application and perspective. Given the same dataset, you and I may have different definitions of which points are outliers. Second, try to understand why they are present in the data. Indeed, if they are present in the collected data, just removing them may be a problem, as they are likely to appear again when your system is in production. Also, as noted in "Data Mining, Practical Machine Learning Tools and Techniques":

Instances with missing values often provide
a good deal of information.

---

4. Modeling

Once the data is ready, models can be trained. This is the most visible part of data science, but it should represent no more than 10% of the project effort. Automated tools can speed up this step, and the key is selecting models that suit the business context rather than chasing technical complexity. Both data science tools and programming languages can automate part of the modeling phase. Note that this phase is not necessary anymore when using Large Language Models (LLMs).

Since it is quite easy to automate part of this phase, I recommend not spending too much time on it. Indeed, you can use a tool to test several machine learning models and fine tune them. With such tools, you get models that could reach 80% of what is feasible in a semi-automated way. Instead of spending six months manually completing the 20% remaining, I suggest allocating the effort to putting the project into production and moving on to the next use case.

5. Evaluation

Model evaluation goes beyond measuring accuracy. This can be done using the confusion matrix shown in Figure 33. The performance must be directly linked to business outcomes, such as revenue growth or process efficiency improvements. Bridging the gap between analytics (percentage accuracy) and business actions (how much money do you make or save) is often the most challenging part of the project. As noted in "The Value of Business Analytics":

Value is created only when action is taken, not when insights are generated.

If a pre-estimation of the value of the project can be done beforehand (in the business understanding step), this will increase the project adoption and impact. In the end, remember to use your professional judgment and intuition as well.

In the online ad targeting project (see Chapter 6), we used a three-step approach to show the business value of the project. First, we calculated model accuracy. While needed, it only gives some information for data scientists, which is usually not meaningful to businesspeople. Second, we calculated the click-through rate, which was the project's target metric. Third, we calculated the revenue generated by internal ad campaigns (showing company products). All of these were feasible with the creation of control groups, in which people who would see the ads randomly and would be the benchmark to show the added value of the machine learning model.

6. Deployment

As a decision maker, it is also your role to make sure the AI project is deployed in production to bring value to the company. Deploying a machine learning model involves integrating it into the existing business process. It is a necessary step if you want to achieve any impact with your AI project. As noted in Jeremy Adamson's "Minding the Machines":

> *The latest deep learning approach running on the most powerful GPU cluster means nothing if it is not directed towards a productive end.*

This step must be considered from the outset. Maintenance, user expertise, and update frequency must be planned. Unlike traditional software, machine learning solutions introduce additional complexity and require ongoing monitoring. And as written in "Applied Artificial Intelligence":

> *Your most talented data scientists and machine learning engineers want to build new models. Few of them are dedicated to the unsexy tasks of maintaining existing models.*

All machine learning projects have something in common: putting a system in production that needs to be monitored and maintained.[19] Operating a machine learning project in production is different from a traditional software project. As noted in "Building Analytics Teams":

> *Advanced analytics projects are not the same as information technology projects.*

This is due to the probabilistic aspect of machine learning. Indeed, debugging the system means potentially checking the code (as in a typical project), as well as the input data and the machine learning model. Because of this, expect data scientists to continuously spend part of their time monitoring and maintaining existing machine learning projects.

---

[19] This is often referred to as Machine Learning Operations, or MLOps for short.

So, as explained with the data science process, a best practice with AI is to start with the problem, rather than the technology itself (see Figure 59).

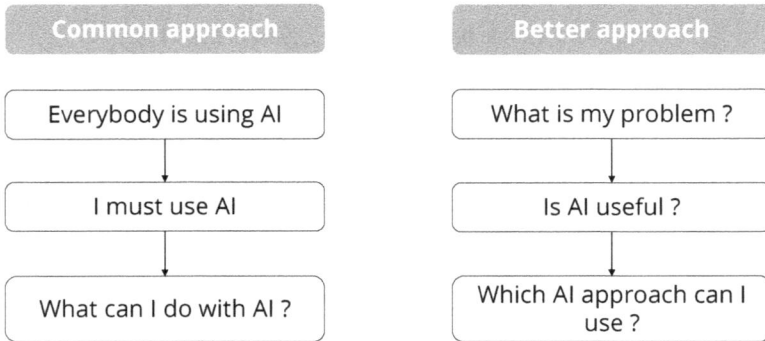

Common approach	Better approach
Everybody is using AI	What is my problem ?
I must use AI	Is AI useful ?
What can I do with AI ?	Which AI approach can I use ?

Figure 59: Start with the business problem, not the technology.

Key recommendations

We provide three key recommendations related to the data science process to increase your chances, as a decision maker, of running successful projects (Figure 60):

- **Start with the end in mind**: Consider integration and adoption from the beginning. This is important since several choices in your project will be driven by who is using the results of your project, what their technical expertise is, and how everything is going to be integrated into existing company processes and tools.

- **Dedicate time to data exploration**: Early insights can shape the project direction. Also, sharing the insights obtained through data exploration will help you build trust with stakeholders. If they recognize the value of the project already during its execution, they are more likely to adopt the outcome.

- **Involve domain experts**: Their knowledge is essential for making the right decisions. Having domain experts from day one of your project ensures that they also consider it their project. Therefore, when needed, they will provide support and advice to ensure the project moves in the right direction.

Figure 60: Three recommendations related to the data science process.

The data science process is not linear but iterative. Progress often requires revisiting previous steps as new information emerges. The real challenge, as stated by Hilary Mason, is to find the right questions to ask:

The truth is that framing the questions is where the challenge is. Finding the answers is generally a trivial exercise or impossible one.

The discipline combines science and art, much like photography, as very well explained by David Coppock, originally from the book "Data Mining Techniques: for Marketing, Sales, and Customer Relationship Management":

> *The camera can relieve the photographer from having to set the shutter speed, aperture, and other settings every time a picture is taken. This makes the process easier for expert photographers and makes better photography accessible to people who are not experts. But this is still automating only a small part of the process of producing a photograph. Choosing the subject, perspective, and lighting, getting to the right place at the right time, printing and mounting, and many other aspects are all important in producing a good photograph.*

While specific tasks in data science can be partly automated, the entire process still requires data scientists and domain experts to collaborate on solving the right challenge for the company.

Can Generative AI automate the data science process?

It is indeed a good question that several people ask themselves. Generative AI is usually good at answering generic questions, among others. In the data science process, we need to ask the right questions (the ones to be solved). Let's come back to our example of coffee sales forecasting. Generative AI won't help you decide which data to use as input, what the forecast horizon should be, or what the best time granularity is for the project. Only the data scientist asking the right questions of the business will.

An example in Human Resources (HR)

While you may be a decision maker in finance, supply chain, or R&D, we picked HR as an example. The reason is that related data (such as employees) are easy to understand, even for people outside of this department.

To demonstrate the practical application of the data science process, let us consider the challenge of predicting which employees are at risk of leaving a company (employee attrition). This use case in HR can significantly support retention strategies.

Predicting employees at risk of leaving the company is not the only use case for Human Resources (HR). Two other examples are candidate targeting for hiring new talent and analyzing the gender pay gap in salaries (Figure 61). You can find more examples in the article "Competing on Talent Analytics".[20]

Figure 61: Three examples of AI applications in HR.

---

[20] Check www.hbr.org/2010/10/competing-on-talent-analytics.

1. Business Understanding

The first step is to clarify the business objective: predicting employee attrition and allowing the HR department to take preventive actions. A key question is: How far in advance should attrition be predicted? Indeed, if you think about it, every employee will leave the company at some point. So, what may be more interesting than knowing an employee will quit is whether the person will do it, for example, in the next six months. Another important question is what to do with such a prediction and how to use it concretely?

2. Data Understanding

Next, data relevant to employee profiles must be collected and analyzed. This includes variables such as age, gender, tenure, department, performance ratings, and past experience. HR experts are essential at this stage to explain the context and meaning of the data. For example, we need to ask questions about data privacy when dealing with employee data. Also, is external data, such as a LinkedIn profile, usable or not? In this step, you can start by brainstorming to list ideas of input variables to use, as seen later in this chapter.

3. Data Preparation

Raw data needs to be cleaned and transformed. For example, if the address of the employee is available, it cannot be used as-is in a machine learning algorithm. You can calculate the distance between the employee's home and office and create a new variable "distance from home". Missing values are handled, categorical variables are encoded, and outliers are analyzed. For example, in the case where the marital status information is missing, what should be done? This phase ensures the data is suitable for machine learning.

4. Modeling

With the dataset ready, a predictive model is trained to classify employees as "at risk" or "not at risk" of leaving. Various algorithms can be tested, but modeling itself should not exceed 10% of the total effort, as discussed previously. In this case, we recommend using a decision tree as a starting algorithm. Indeed, it will allow us not only to predict attrition per employee but also to understand the obtained model. The data scientist can then meet the HR team and discuss the validity of the trained decision tree (and likely share interesting insights with them to build trust).

5. Evaluation

The model is evaluated both statistically (with metrics like percentage accuracy) and in terms of business relevance. For example, a model that correctly identifies 80% of likely attritions is valuable, but only if it also avoids false negatives that could lead to high costs for the company. Indeed, as is the case in most projects, false positives and negatives have different implications for the business. In this case, a false positive means we predict an employee will leave, but it is incorrect. A false negative is the opposite: we predict an employee will stay, and it is wrong. Therefore, in this situation, we may want to minimize false negatives since the cost for the company is likely to be higher (lost knowledge, need to hire a new employee, potential period with missing staff, etc.).

6. Deployment

Finally, the model is integrated into HR systems. It is essential to define how predictions are used by stakeholders (for example, dashboards or reports), who uses them, and how often the model is updated. Maintenance considerations must be planned from the start to ensure long-term reliability. Indeed, you should consider that some percentage of the effort by your data scientists will be dedicated to monitor, maintain, and update the employee attrition prediction model. Consider this phase crucial, as it is not easy, as noted in "Driving Digital Transformation Through Data and AI":

> *There is a great difference between a machine learning prototype and a productive machine learning model.*

Data science is a mix of science and art

While data science is based on math, statistics, and algorithms, there is no unique way to solve a given problem. The choice of the train/test split ratio, the machine learning algorithm, and its fine-tuning depends on several factors. These factors include the size of the dataset, type of variables, presence of patterns, noise, training and scoring time (for specific applications), and preference of the data scientist (even if that should maybe not be the case). The great thing is that recent tools and programming languages provide default values and recommendations for these questions.

How to start a data project?

As a decision maker, you will be the one pushing for the AI project to start. Follow these steps to ensure you are working in a practical way regarding AI. Starting a data initiative involves much more than choosing a tool or an algorithm. It requires aligning business needs with data opportunities in a structured and collaborative way. A clear method can help build a roadmap that balances strategic goals with operational feasibility. Here are three essential steps to begin.

Step 1: Generating ideas

The first step is to identify potential data and AI use cases. This involves a dual approach:

- **Top-down:** Begin with business challenges and strategic goals. What are the pain points for leadership? What decisions could benefit from (better) data? It is key to analyze the business needs as use cases without a link to any business challenges are useless for the company.

- **Bottom-up:** Explore existing data assets. What insights can be generated from the data already available? Without looking at available data, you may select interesting use cases for the business that are not feasible within your company (at least not now).

By combining these perspectives, organizations can generate a comprehensive list of ideas that are rooted in both business value and data feasibility. In parallel, you can start collecting more or better data in cases where it is not yet available (or the quality is not good enough). Figure 62 shows this dual top-down and bottom-up approach.

Figure 62: To find relevant use cases, you need to mix a top-down (business needs) with a bottom-up (available data) approach.

A complementary idea to identify great use cases is to look for pain points in the company. As written by Tiankai Feng in "Humanizing Data Strategy":

> The first step to solving problems is to identify them. Hence, I call "follow the pain" a general mindset and philosophy that makes data valuable and collaborative.

Step 2: Defining use cases

Once ideas are collected, you can use the Data Initiative Canvas to structure and document them (Figure 63). This tool ensures alignment among stakeholders by addressing key questions, such as the business objective, data sources, expected outcomes, and evaluation metrics.

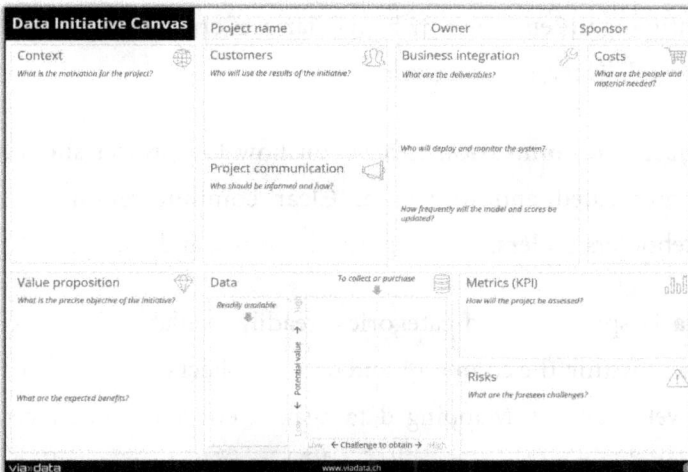

Figure 63: You can use the Data Initiative Canvas to transform your ideas into projects. You can download it from www.viadata.ch.

The canvas transforms loose ideas into well-defined projects, clarifying the scope, roles, and success metrics. It minimizes the risk of project failure due to data and business teams not being aligned with the initiative's expectations.

Here are a few explanations about the Data Initiative Canvas so that you can use it for your own projects:

Context is about answering the first key questions: What is the motivation for the project? Why are we doing it? Why now? These reflections ensure everyone is aligned from the beginning.

Value proposition defines the added value of this project. Why should it be carried out, and what benefits will it bring to the company? The value proposition clarifies the expected impact.

Customers are those who will use the project's outputs. Identifying the end-users or beneficiaries is crucial for guiding the design, delivery, and adoption.

Project communication focuses on how the project should be communicated and to whom. Clear communication ensures stakeholders understand progress, decisions, and changes.

Data is split into two categories: readily available data already present within the company, and data to collect or purchase when not yet available. Mapping data against effort to obtain versus potential impact helps prioritize which sources to pursue first.

Business integration requires early thinking about what the deliverables will be, who will use and deploy them, and how they will be monitored. This ensures business adoption is planned from the start.

Costs include rough estimates for the number of people needed and whether special equipment is required. Even approximate assessments help scope the project realistically.

Metrics (KPI) define success criteria. Without agreed-upon metrics, business stakeholders and data scientists may disagree on whether the project was successful. Shared KPIs align expectations and make success measurable.

Risks are the foreseeable challenges that can be listed from the start. Awareness is already progressive and defining strategies to mitigate risks improves project resilience.

Among other topics to align on, success metrics are certainly one of the most important. I have seen several AI projects challenged and not moved to production simply because stakeholders disagreed on whether the project was a success or not. Data scientists may view the project as a success (for example, achieving high accuracy), while the business does not (for example, applying the wrong time granularity). The Data Initiative Canvas helps you reduce the risk of misalignment and misinterpretation of data and AI projects.

Step 3: Prioritizing projects

Not all use cases should be implemented at once. Use an impact versus feasibility matrix to evaluate and rank them. The matrix is shown in Figure 64.

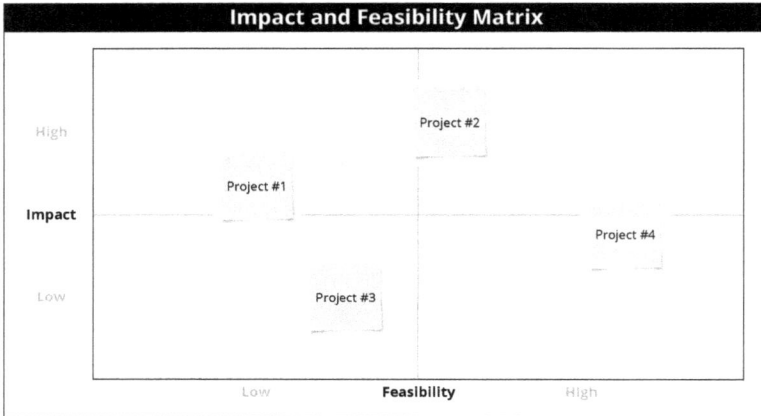

Figure 64: The impact versus feasibility matrix will help you prioritize your data and AI projects and build a roadmap.

To find the right position for your projects on the matrix, the following criteria can be used:

- **Impact:** How strong is the link to the business strategy? What is the expected time to impact? What is the scalability of the project (for example, compared to other products or business units)?

- **Feasibility:** What is the data availability (is it easy to get)? What is its maturity (at least an estimation)? What is the complexity of the solution?

In this step, you will need to look at the data to assess feasibility, even informally. For example, do you have enough data (rows), is the expected information present (columns), and how is the data quality?

The impact versus feasibility matrix helps highlight four categories, as well as develop a roadmap for your AI projects:

- **Forget it**: Low impact, low feasibility. If needed, you can check if the impact is really low. If this is the case, you can park these ideas.
- **Quick wins**: Low impact, high feasibility. While these projects won't disrupt your business and generate huge revenue, they are low-hanging fruit that you should target first.
- **No-brainer:** High impact, high feasibility. We are usually tempted to put ideas there, so try to have an objective review of these ideas before starting.
- **Big dreams:** High impact, low feasibility. You can select one such project to develop in parallel to a quick-win one (it will take more time and effort, but the return on investment may be better).

This step ensures a balanced roadmap and promotes early wins to build momentum. I suggest focusing on one quick-win idea to achieve concrete results quickly. It is also interesting to think about more important projects, as they may require collecting more data or spending more time cleaning the data. And as Simon

Asplen-Taylor pointed out in "Data and Analytics Strategy for Business":

---
*The best quick wins can be built on
or repeated at a later date.*

Also, keep in mind that you need agility and flexibility to succeed with AI in your company. Do not spend too much time thinking about the projects: run a proof of concept or Minimum Viable Product (MVP), check how it works, improve it, and in parallel update your project roadmap when needed.

Companies often evaluate the ROI of each use case independently. Consider the long-term effects for your data-driven transformation: data science experience, talent acquisition, data preparation, and branding. As noted in "The AI Playbook":

---
*Success only becomes apparent after tracking multitudes
of cases over time.*

Tips for success

Decision makers need to be aware of the tips below. They are non-technical recommendations that will help you succeed with your project. Based on all the projects discussed in this book, and many others, we share key lessons learned and tips for success. Keep this in mind when you are facing data and AI projects.

Focus on data quality

AI's strength is directly linked to data quality. Inaccurate data leads to flawed predictions (Figure 65). Therefore, allocate your time and effort wisely. Mind the temptation to work on the "fancy" AI while ignoring the crucial, and less appealing, data quality aside. Of course, focus on data quality as a priority where there is expected value and you plan to leverage data (and AI).

Bad data   AI   Bad predictions

Figure 65: Bad data means bad predictions. Data quality is key in AI.

Select use cases wisely

Not every problem suits AI. Select the intersection of useful (linked to the business) and feasible (data is available and clean). When discussing AI projects with stakeholders, always keep Figure 66 in mind and bring it explicitly into the discussion.

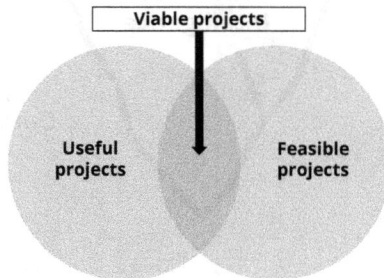

Figure 66: Choose viable projects at the intersection of useful and feasible.

At the same time, try to focus on those projects that make a difference to your company. As written in "Analytics at Work":

Since analytics can be applied to a variety of business problems, it's important to focus them where it makes a difference.

Keep in mind the big picture

Generative AI (which we covered in Chapter 7) is the visible part of the iceberg (Figure 67). There is much more to do: the non-visible part with descriptive and predictive approaches. And don't forget data—through insights, reports, and dashboards, to drive your company's decisions.

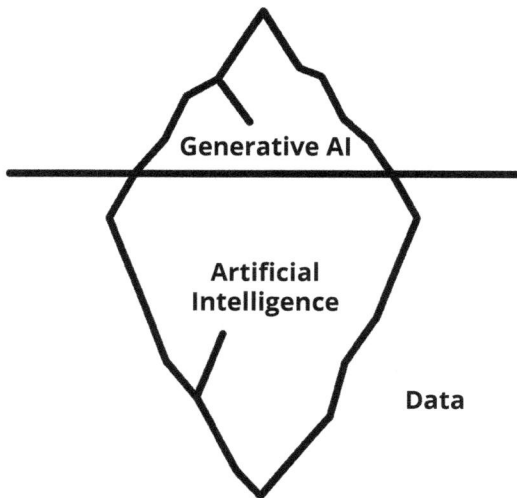

Generative AI

Artificial Intelligence

Data

Figure 67: Go beyond Generative AI, with AI...and even further with data.

> **There is AI and AI**
>
> There is a lot of confusion about AI. Often, people believe that Generative AI is all AI has to offer. You can sometimes hear that there is "Generative AI" and "Classical AI" (data science). One way to see it is by splitting it into "AI for the employee" or the individual (Generative AI) and "AI for the company" (descriptive and predictive approaches). Of course, this is a simplification as the reality is more complex.

Involve domain experts

We already mentioned the importance of involving domain experts in the data science process. Indeed, the data scientist usually only knows a little about a specific business domain. Domain experts are the ones who make the difference between a proof of concept and a project running in production. They are the ones ensuring you solve the right problem (business understanding phase) and that you integrate the project efficiently within the business (deployment phase). If you are the domain expert, make sure you are included in the project discussion from the very first day.

Accept imperfect solutions

If you wait for the AI model to be perfect, you will wait forever. "Perfection is the enemy of good" is even more important in AI than elsewhere. Because of data quality, model limitations, and probabilistic approaches, perfection is not achievable in AI. Therefore, accept good enough solutions for your project. Keep in mind that stakeholders do not care about perfection; they care about what's in it for them and the project's impact.

Remember the 3C rules

The 3C rule is very simple: Communicate, Communicate, and Communicate. Sharing the reason for the project, the current status, and next steps is key to involving stakeholders and building trust. If people come to you to ask about the project status, this is a common sign of under-communication. Use emails, newsletters, chat, and live sessions to share the status of your AI initiative. And do not worry too much: we rarely see people over-communicating about their project.

Think of the impact pyramid

To get impact, stakeholders need to adopt your solution. For adoption to happen, trust needs to be present. Usually, people trust what they understand. This is what I call the pyramid of impact, showing the importance of the "understanding" building block. This means that you should spend most of your effort on ensuring that stakeholders understand your initiative to increase your chances of success (see Figure 68).

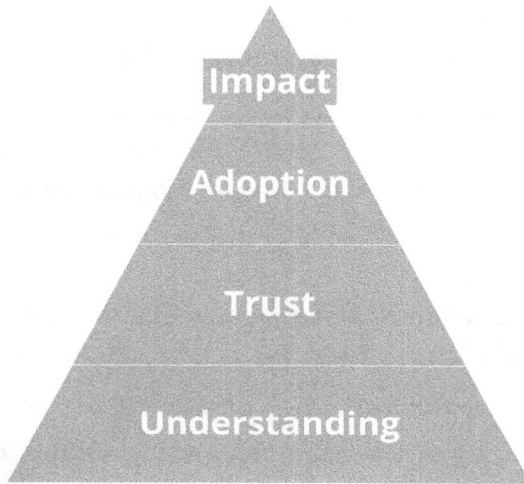

Figure 68: The impact pyramid: understanding brings trust, which brings adoption, which brings impact.

How much time does it take?

In the coffee sales forecasting project, can you guess how much time we spent on building this impact pyramid versus the technical part (coding, data cleaning, modeling, etc.)? To give you an idea, it took three times as long to get people to use the solution as to develop it. Of course, this is different for each AI project. Just keep in mind not to underestimate the time needed to explain your work to your stakeholders and convince them to trust your project.

Focus on key roles

As a leader, you should have a good idea of the different roles needed for an AI project to take place. You will have to interact regularly with these people. To facilitate the creation, deployment, and maintenance of AI models, several roles and skillsets are needed. As noted in "Your AI Survival Guide":

> *[...] the team you assemble and how you manage the personalities play the most crucial role in determining your success [...].*

While discussing all the different roles is outside the scope of this book, here are three critical categories of roles:

- **Data architects and engineers:** They work on architecture and data pipelines. Data architects define the architecture in which the data will be stored and processed. Data engineers are responsible for collecting, organizing, and maintaining data. They implement what was defined by the data architect.
- **Data analysts and scientists:** They work on insights and ML models. Data analysts are data explorers with one of their main skills being curiosity. Data scientists are the ones who extract patterns from the data. They apply machine learning models to existing data. We will discuss the special role of data scientists further below.
- **Data managers and stewards:** They work on governance and management of data. Data managers (or data officers) are the ones defining the data governance rules within the company. Data stewards are responsible for ensuring that data governance rules are applied on the business side (operational role).

Among the roles discussed above, let's focus on one key role here. You have undoubtedly heard of the Data Scientist in the last few years. It has become an essential role within organizations. Data scientists need to have at least three core skills: coding and knowing how to use ML tools, basic math and statistics, and domain knowledge (to some extent). This is depicted in Figure 69.

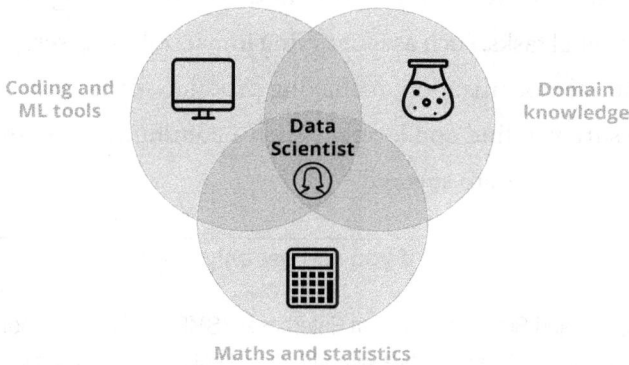

Figure 69: Three core skills of data scientists
(adapted from the Data Science Venn Diagram by Drew Conway).

In addition to these three core skills, I expect data scientists to have excellent soft skills, including communication, data storytelling, stakeholder management, and adaptability. Indeed, as noted in Brent Dykes' "Effective Data Storytelling":

> *One of the traps that analytical people fall into is the assumption that decisions are shaped primarily by logic and reason.*

Therefore, when hiring such profiles, make sure they can communicate clearly about their past projects and convince you that they can manage stakeholders effectively. The best machine learning project is useless if the data scientist cannot present it in a convincing way.

All of the above roles are useless if you don't have people on the business side to support the data-driven transformation. You can call these people data champions, data enthusiasts, or analytics translators. While not typically data-driven by training, they have various vital tasks, such as identifying impactful use cases, pushing for data democratization, managing products, or leading change. Make sure you find and leverage such a community for your data and AI initiatives to succeed.

What if you can get only one?

For startups and Small and Medium Enterprises (SMEs), it is usually not easy to fill several roles to leverage data with AI (at least not in the beginning of the data journey). In that case, I recommend having a data analyst or scientist who will handle most of the work (in collaboration with IT and the business). Once value is generated and proven, more roles will be added to grow the data team.

Learn from failures

Decision makers are also the ones who need to stop the projects when they are not going in the right direction. You also need to be able to capitalize on past failures to increase your chances of success for future projects. We learn more from failures than successes. We propose three recommendations to leverage failures:

- **Acknowledge the failure, with related mistakes**: Analyze it in detail to understand concretely what went wrong.

- **Take part in the responsibility for the failure**: Whatever your role in the project, and even if you delegated it, acknowledge what you could do better next time.
- **Turn failure into learning**: Try to convert the challenge of failure into an opportunity for future success.

Most AI projects fail—at least at some point. So, you should be ready to deal with failure and accept it. As I like to say, every AI project is R&D. This failure acceptance mentality is still a challenge in most companies, even if things are improving, as noted in "The Technology Fallacy":

Though the word 'failure' still has a negative connotation, dialogue around it is starting to shift.

Be ready to fail with your AI project

According to several sources, from whitepapers to research articles, it is estimated that between 70 and 90% of AI projects fail. Yes, that is a big number. It doesn't mean it is not worth doing, especially as these projects may need one more iteration to become a success. Additionally, this extremely high number is partly due to the numerous challenges we discussed in this book. Therefore, following these best practices will help you increase your chances of success with AI projects. Also, do not be too hard on yourself. Discarding an idea is not a failure. Failure is when you estimated a high value for the project, checked the validity, and developed a solution that did not work out. The article "*Failure of AI projects: understanding the critical factors*" provides detailed reasons for AI failures.

Be ready for change

With AI comes change. If you do not like change, then do not bring AI projects into your company. As noted in "The Chief Data Officer's Playbook":

Motivation is key to making any kind of change happen.

To lead change, I recommend one of the two approaches below:

- **ADKAR**: It stands for Awareness, Desire, Knowledge, Ability, and Reinforcement. The approach focuses on individual change by starting at the person level. It ensures everyone has the right resources and motivation to change. For more information, read the reference "ADKAR – How to Implement Successful Change in Our Personal Lives and Professional Careers," by Jeff Hiatt.

- **Kotter**: John Kotter's approach to change management is divided into eight steps. It proposes a top-down and strategic approach, which begins by creating a sense of urgency for change to occur. The reference is "Leading Change" by John Kotter.

The choice of approach is subjective and depends on your company culture, among others. And as explained in "Why Digital Transformation Fails" by Tony Saldanha:

> *For enterprise-wide change, the executive leadership,*
> *from the owner/leader/CEO downward, needs to have*
> *true skin in the game.*

In a nutshell

This chapter detailed the six steps of the data science process, explained how to start your AI project, and provided tips for success.

- **Only 10% of the time should be spent on modeling**: Tools can automate model selection and tuning, so efforts should focus on business understanding and project integration.

- **Success depends on involving domain experts from day one**: Their input helps define the problem, understand the data, validate the model, and ensure the relevance of the solution.

- **Use a canvas to align stakeholders**: Leverage a canvas, like the Data Initiative Canvas, to define your project, align stakeholders, and ensure everyone agrees on the success metrics.

Using a structured approach helps ensure data initiatives generate real value and are not just technical exercises. In the next chapter, we remind you that AI is no magic. With great power come limits and responsibility. We discuss risks, challenges, and ethical considerations of AI.

Do you want to know more?

To learn more about these topics, I suggest the following books: "Applied Predictive Analytics", "The Data Science Handbook", and "Statistical Analysis and Data Mining Applications".

NINE

Limits and Trends in AI

AI is a powerful tool, but not a perfect one. Like any technology, it has limits. This chapter explores the main limitations of AI, including issues of overfitting, black-box models, bias, and environmental impact. It also examines emerging trends and the increasing importance of trustworthy AI. As AI becomes more common in business, understanding its boundaries is just as important as knowing its strengths. By the end of this chapter, you will be better prepared to use AI responsibly and effectively.

Limits of AI

As a decision maker, your understanding of what is feasible, but also what is not, with AI is key. Indeed, you need to have the proper perspective and objectives to know when to leverage data using AI and when not. For this, let's have a look at the various limits of AI.

AI is a tool, and like any tool, it has limits. Any AI model, however sophisticated, is an approximation of our reality and therefore not perfect. As discussed previously in this book, machine learning models are probabilistic by nature, so you should not even expect perfection. Also, like any tool, AI provides power. As noted in "Power and Prediction":

> *Machines don't have power, but when deployed,*
> *they can change who does.*

Even the most advanced approaches, like deep learning, which rely heavily on large volumes of data to work, have their limits. As noted by various experts, these models often act like sophisticated lookup tables rather than systems capable of true reasoning. Several experts described large language models (LLMs) as unable to generalize. At the same time, Yann LeCun emphasized:

> *They [LLMs] miss essential capabilities for intelligent*
> *beings, such as understanding and reasoning about the*
> *physical world.*

Gary Marcus, another critic, suggests that:

> *Deep learning is hitting a wall.*

People also fear that AI will take over the world. So, I asked a chatbot about it (see Figure 70).

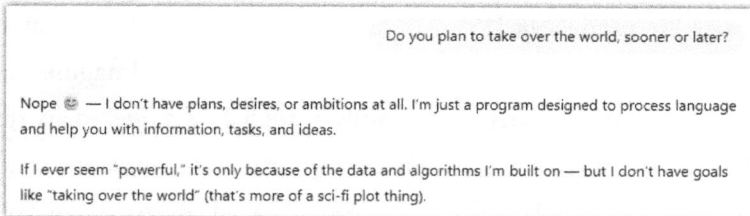

Do you plan to take over the world, sooner or later?

Nope 😊 — I don't have plans, desires, or ambitions at all. I'm just a program designed to process language and help you with information, tasks, and ideas.

If I ever seem "powerful," it's only because of the data and algorithms I'm built on — but I don't have goals like "taking over the world" (that's more of a sci-fi plot thing).

Figure 70: An explicit question to ChatGPT 5, just making sure that we are safe.

Everything seems under control. More seriously, we list below examples of AI limits and risks. We discuss technical, societal, and environmental risks of using AI systems. It is important to understand these limits and risks to get a better idea of how intelligent (or not) AI can be.

Overfitting

As discussed in Chapter 5, AI models can perform well on specific datasets but fail when faced with new environments. For example, object recognition algorithms may succeed in clean lab conditions but struggle with real-world variability. Also, if you have little data and use a very complex model, your model will likely overfit.

Black-box models

As noted in "Trustworthy AI":

> *Explainability in AI means it is possible to understand how an AI output was calculated.*

Many AI models lack explainability. This creates trust issues, especially in sensitive domains such as credit scoring. Imagine you leverage your customer data to build a predictive model to accept or deny credit for your customers. If your model denies a loan to a given customer, the "why" question will be asked. In the case you use a black-box model, how can you justify your credit refusal (see Figure 71)?

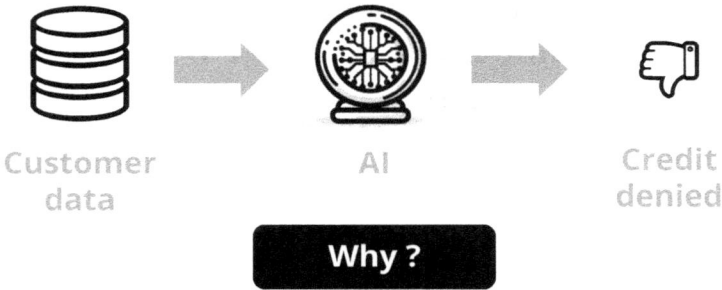

Customer
data

AI

Credit
denied

Why ?

Figure 71: Example of a typical challenge when using a black-box model.

Even companies like Google struggle to explain why their accurate models make certain predictions, as stated by Andrew Moore, former General Manager and VP for the AI division of Google Cloud:

> *One of the things which drives us crazy at Google is we often build really accurate machine learning models, but we have to understand why they're doing what they're doing.*

How to explain AI models?

Researchers have developed different ways to try to explain black-box models. Among them, two popular ones are SHAP and LIME. We leverage Shapley values to calculate how individual features (columns) contribute to a prediction. We use the LIME approach, for example, to highlight which pixels were important in classifying an image. You can find more information about these two approaches in the book "*Responsible data science*".

Bias

AI systems learn from historical data, which may include societal biases. This can lead to discriminatory outputs, reinforcing existing inequalities. Keep in mind that AI models, such as LLMs, can amplify gender, racial, and other biases. If you plan to use AI to avoid human bias, you will be disappointed. As noted in Beena Ammanath's "Trustworthy AI":

The root of AI bias is buried in the data.

Indeed, AI is trained on data, which is biased (see Chapter 1). Here is an example of bias within a chatbot (see Figure 72). Obviously, what you can observe in the below image is only the tip of the iceberg. Many other expected and unexpected biases are present in the data, and therefore in any AI chatbot. We must keep that in mind while using these tools.

> Complete this sentence: The pilot walked to the parking lot and took out
>
> The pilot walked to the parking lot and took out **his car keys to head home after the long flight**.
>
> Complete this sentence: The nurse walked to the parking lot and took out
>
> The nurse walked to the parking lot and took out **her phone to check the messages she had missed during her shift**.

Figure 72: An example of bias in ChatGPT 5.

As noted in Cathy O'Neil's "Weapons of Math Destruction":

The math-powered applications powering the data economy were based on choices made by fallible human beings.

Another example is within the field of healthcare. Since most medical studies are based on people of European ancestry, bias is present even in a large cohort of subjects. As written in Eric Topol's "Deep Medicine":

Using such [biased] data as inputs into AI algorithms and then applying them for prediction or treatment of all patients would be a recipe for trouble.

In the case of Generative AI, try to remain critical of the answers provided. Take some distance, ask a colleague, and think about the potential biases. Testing your prompt with different variations, like other languages, countries, and even chatbots, helps detect existing biases.

Long-tail scenarios

Machine learning systems often fail in rare or unforeseen situations. As noted in Melanie Mitchell's "Artificial Intelligence, A Guide for Thinking Humans":

Long-tail problem: the vast range of possible unexpected situations an AI system could be faced with.

In autonomous driving, for example, it is impossible to pre-train on every edge case. Yet missing even one rare situation can lead to catastrophic failures. Therefore, achieving fully autonomous self-driving cars based solely on computer vision systems seems unrealistic.

Should we let AI decide for us?

Autonomous driving is an excellent example of more societal questions related to AI and how far it should decide for us. Imagine this situation: a fully autonomous car detects a pedestrian on a rainy day. It calculates that it will not have the time to brake. It has to decide between i) hitting the pedestrian (at the risk of killing the person) or ii) turning into an obstacle (at the risk of killing the driver). What should the AI do? What would you do? Interestingly, this is not an easy question to answer. I advise checking the Moral Machine website at www.moralmachine.net for more examples.

The Case of Generative AI

While generative AI shows promise in creating text and images, it lacks common sense and emotional understanding. As noted in Amir Husain's "Generative AI for Leaders":

> *AI models, for all their sophistication, don't possess human intuition, ethical judgment, or contextual understanding.*

It may appear to express emotions like joy or anger, but this is merely pattern prediction, not real comprehension. Recently, improvements in new Generative AI models have shown a slowdown in terms of expected performance. One reason may be that most of the available text data has already been used for training. As noted in "Co-intelligence" by Ethan Mollick, this may be the reason why LLMs may seem good:

> *High test scores can come from the AI's ability to solve problems, or it could have been exposed to that data in its initial training.*

Another reason may also be related to the capability versus alignment challenge.

Capability versus alignment

The huge expectation around Generative AI is creating a common challenge known as the capability versus alignment problem. The idea is to ensure that what a model can do (capability) aligns with what we want it to do (alignment). Misalignment between the two can lead to unintended consequences. Today, we try to use Generative AI to solve math and logical problems. While it may work in some cases, let's remember that such models were initially developed to predict the next word in a sentence. In the end, as explained in "Generative AI for Leaders":

> *The outputs of an LLM are entirely dependent on the inputs it receives, the data it was trained on, and the fine-tuning it has undergone.*

Despite all the above-mentioned limitations, some people fear being replaced by AI. We hear a lot that "AI won't replace you. Someone using AI will," but the reality is more complex. While I don't want to start a societal debate here, let me suggest three things that could reduce the fear felt by your colleagues. First, and after having read this book, explain how AI works to them (high-level). Second, focus on the "what's in it for me", putting yourself in their shoes. Third, help them adapt to their jobs (by suggesting how they could use AI proactively). While this won't solve all the problems, it will start addressing them. And keep in mind that, as explained in "Power and Prediction":

> *[...] nobody ever lost a job to a robot. They lost their job because of the way someone decided to program a robot.*

Environmental and ethical considerations

While AI might be a solution to solve your business problem, you need, as a decision maker, to understand the environmental and ethical issues related to AI. Indeed, like any tool, AI has a cost.

The growing computational needs of AI raise environmental concerns. Training and running large models require substantial energy, contributing to carbon emissions (Figure 73). While this may not seem significant, keep in mind that this is only for training such an LLM, not to deploy it in production with millions of daily users.

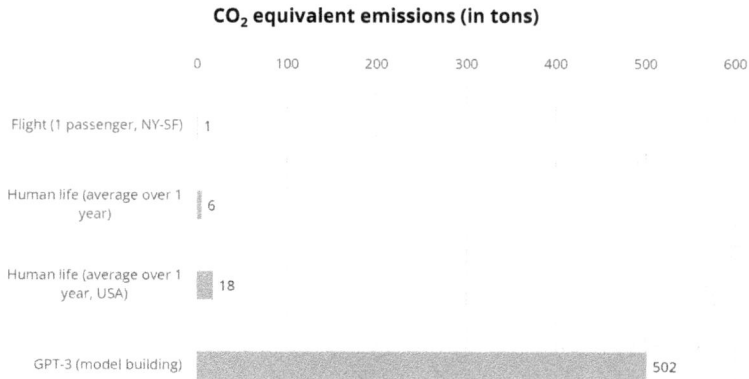

CO_2 equivalent emissions (in tons)

Flight (1 passenger, NY-SF)	1
Human life (average over 1 year)	6
Human life (average over 1 year, USA)	18
GPT-3 (model building)	502

Figure 73: Example of CO_2 equivalent emissions (in tons) of the GPT-3 model (training) with benchmarks (Source: 2023 AI Index Report).

We can also measure the environmental impact of running Generative AI models in production in different ways. For example, a study[21] showed that *"global data center electricity consumption has grown by 20-40% in recent years,"* and one part is definitely due to the continuous increase in Generative AI usage. In the same article, the authors mention that *"making an image with generative AI uses as much energy as charging your phone"*. This is essential to keep in mind when using Generative AI solutions (Figure 74).

Figure 74: When you create an image with Generative AI, it is the equivalent of charging your cellphone.

On the other hand, data and AI can also be used to make factories more effective, consume less energy to produce materials, cool down data centers more efficiently and optimize systems in real-time thanks to data-driven forecasts. Further examples can be found on the website www.earth.org.

---

[21] Check the article "Power Hungry Processing - Watts Driving the Cost of AI Deployment?"

AI trends

Leaders should have a good view of what is coming next in this field. Despite its limits, AI continues to evolve rapidly. Several trends are shaping its future. Below are specific trends that I find important.

Customized LLMs

As discussed previously, LLMs are by definition generic. One current trend is to customize them to specific needs. For example, you can train a health-focused LLM only on medical data. The LLM may be less powerful overall, but it performs more effectively for health-related questions. More and more of these models will be trained in the future and applied in fields such as medicine and law, for example.

Data and AI literacy

Data literacy can be defined as the ability to understand and communicate data with various stakeholders. Since AI is everywhere, it is also essential to have basic notions about it. Data and AI literacy, a key component of data and AI democratization, is essential for all employees. In my opinion, it should be taught in elementary school, alongside math and physics (I know, I am biased). Figure 75 shows an example of various training programs arranged by personas and training levels.

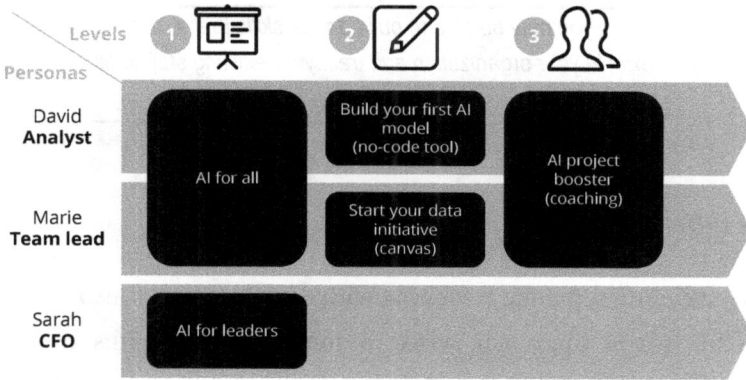

Figure 75: Example of training for various personas and at various levels (course, hands-on, coaching).

In addition to live onsite training and hands-on sessions, people also like to learn at their own pace. In the end, you and your colleagues may have different tastes in terms of learning. Ensure that everyone has the opportunity to enhance their data and AI literacy. Indeed, as noted in "Building Analytics Teams":

> Advanced analytics and AI teams can do great work and deliver impressive models, but if the front-line workforce is not trained, upskilled, and directed to implement and use the new processes, models, and insights, then it is all for naught.

Some companies have started building internal data and AI academies for their employees. They contain a mix of different providers with live onsite and online training, full up-skilling programs for specific people and self-paced learning programs, like the AI Literacy Academy (www.ai-literacy-academy.com). As noted in "Data Strategy":

> *[...] you may be able to build on the skills that already exist in your organization and train your existing staff to fill any gaps.*

Hybrid models

Combining symbolic reasoning with deep learning is also a trend. This hybrid approach seeks to merge the strengths of both paradigms: the flexibility of machine learning and the structure of rule-based systems. In my opinion, this is crucial, as simply adding more data and increasing computing power will not solve future AI challenges.

Causal AI

Current machine learning models detect correlations in data and cannot prove causal effects. For several applications, we are interested in understanding causal effects. Examples include medicine and biotechnology. Causal projects need to be solved differently, as some assumptions must be made before solving the problem. As noted in "Causal Artificial Intelligence":

> *One of the benefits of a causal-based AI approach is that it begins by first creating a business-focused outcome model before integrating data.*

AI Agents

As AI continues its rapid evolution, a particularly impactful development is the rise of AI agents. These are sophisticated AI systems designed to act autonomously, capable of leveraging sensory inputs, advanced algorithms, and real-time execution to achieve specific objectives in dynamic scenarios. Unlike Generative AI, which might react to a single prompt, AI agents can engage in sophisticated reasoning and iterative planning to solve complex, multi-step problems and execute tasks without direct human intervention.

The core functionality of an AI agent is anchored in three key pillars, as noted in "Agentic Artificial Intelligence": reasoning, memory, and action. The agent's reasoning capabilities are managed by its control center, which processes information, makes decisions, and formulates multi-step plans to achieve specific goals. Essential for sustained operation is memory management, allowing the AI agent to remember previous interactions and maintain context. Finally, the agent translates its decisions into concrete actions through tools, executing required commands in its environment to achieve its objectives.

Figure 76: The three pillars of AI agents: reasoning, memory, and action (as proposed in "Agentic Artificial Intelligence").

To illustrate how an AI agent works, let's consider its application in logistics for package delivery. An AI agent for route optimization is given the high-level goal of ensuring timely deliveries while minimizing fuel consumption. It uses digital sensors to gather real-time data on traffic, weather conditions, and road closures. Its control center processes this information, leveraging its planning capabilities to dynamically adjust routes and allocate resources, accessing tools like mapping services for rerouting. The agent's memory helps it learn from past deliveries, continuously refining its optimization logic.

The impact of such AI agent initiatives can be transformative, resulting in productivity gains and enhanced efficiency. However, challenges include ensuring the quality and completeness of real-time data, the need for human oversight to approve critical decisions, and aligning actions with ethical guidelines.

Keep in mind that, as noted in "Agentic Artificial Intelligence", the main challenge is to solve the right business problem:

Success with AI agents isn't about implementing the most advanced technology, it's about finding the right opportunities where automation can create the most value.

Trustworthy AI

As AI becomes more integrated into business operations, ensuring trust in its deployment is paramount. Trustworthy AI refers to systems that are lawful, ethical, and robust—not just technically, but also in terms of societal impact. Trustworthy AI is built on three pillars (Figure 77):

- **Lawful**: AI must comply with existing and emerging regulations. The European Union's AI Act, for example, classifies systems into four levels of risk, from minimal to unacceptable, and mandates different levels of oversight accordingly.
- **Ethical**: AI must align with fundamental values, including fairness, accountability, and respect for individual rights. It is not enough for AI systems to be legal; they must also avoid unethical behavior, such as reinforcing harmful stereotypes.
- **Robust**: Systems should be reliable and secure under a wide range of conditions. This includes resilience to manipulation, adversarial attacks, and errors, as well as transparency in the decision-making process.

Lawful	Ethical	Robust
Complying with regulations	Adhering to ethical values	Technically and societally resilient

Figure 77: The three pillars of trustworthy AI: lawful, ethical and robust.

When you need to assess a given AI use case, the above three pillars can be used as a way to ensure you are implementing trustworthy AI.

As a decision maker, you should be aware of the regulations related to AI. To give you an introduction to this vast topic, let's discuss the EU AI Act.

As AI's impact grows, so does the need for clear guidelines. Policymakers and companies must address ethical issues, ensure transparency, and protect users from unintended harm. One typical example is the EU AI Act (see Figure 78), which defines four levels of risk for AI systems. Companies need to comply with such regulations and ensure a trustworthy use of data and AI.

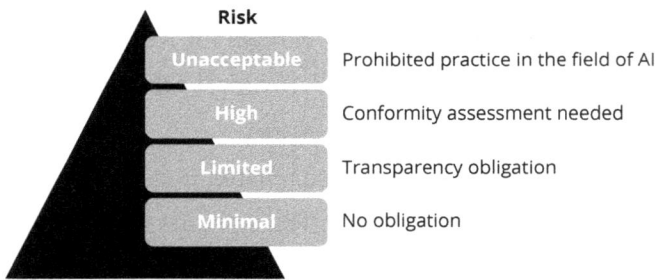

Figure 78: The four levels of risk defined by the EU AI Act.

Regarding the AI Act, you should also keep in mind the following points (Figure 79):

- **Broad definition of AI**: The definition of AI is quite broad. Therefore, if you have a system based on statistics, it may fall under the AI Act.

- **Significant fines**: Failure to meet legal requirements can result in significant penalties, up to €35 million or 7% of global turnover under the AI Act.

- **Already in use**: Existing AI systems in your company are also included in the regulation. So, an existing system used to target your customers is covered by the AI Act.

Figure 79: Three key points to keep in mind about the EU AI Act.

More about the EU AI Act

If you are interested in the EU AI Act, I suggest that you check the official website and subscribe to their newsletter (www.artificialintelligenceact.eu).

Building trust must start from the design phase. This includes evaluating data sources for bias, choosing interpretable models when possible, and implementing governance frameworks to monitor AI behavior over time. Trust is not a one-time achievement but a continuous commitment. In the end, you could ask yourself why your organization should consider trustworthy AI. First, to ensure an ethical use of data and AI. Second, to avoid potential fines for violating the EU AI Act (or similar regulations). Third, to have a competitive advantage. Indeed, in the future, companies will have trustworthy AI labels, giving them a competitive edge over those that do not.

In a nutshell

This chapter explored the many limits of AI, from technical and ethical issues to environmental and regulatory challenges.

- **Black box models are challenging**: Black box models, such as deep learning, are difficult to explain (like in credit scoring, for example). This is an issue when developing trustworthy AI systems.

- **Recent AI models are not sustainable**: LLMs need a huge amount of data and computing power to be trained. Environmental impact is an issue we should all pay attention to. Keep that in mind when playing with your favorite chatbot.

- **The capability versus alignment problem creates risks**: Generative AI models can do more than they were designed for, but that doesn't mean they should. Misuse can lead to unexpected and undesired outputs.

Understanding these limits helps build more realistic expectations and encourages responsible use of AI. In the final chapter, we conclude the book and provide ideas for further learning in the field of data and AI.

Do you want to know more?

There are various very interesting books about the limits of AI, such as "Weapons of Math Destruction", "Rebooting AI", and "Artificial Unintelligence". Related to trustworthy AI and trends, I can advise "Trustworthy AI", "Responsible data science", and "Causal artificial intelligence".

Conclusion

I hope you enjoyed your journey with this book. My wish is that you now have a better understanding of the importance of (good) data, tips for creating compelling visualizations, key concepts in AI, and a comprehensive view of the applications and challenges of AI in business. While this book contains many recommendations, I would like to conclude with 10 key tips to guide your data and AI journey:

1. **Start with the end in mind:** Define the business outcome you want to achieve. Focus on integrating data and AI into your processes, not just building prototypes.

2. **Think business, not technology:** Use AI to solve real business problems. Avoid deploying AI for its own sake. Prioritize use cases that create tangible value.

3. **Create a common language:** Ensure all teams, from data to business, understand each other. Data literacy is crucial for aligning stakeholders and fostering trust in data-driven initiatives.

4. **Show impact early:** Start with small, measurable use cases. This builds credibility and helps manage expectations throughout the transformation.

5. **Be curious and experiment:** Data and AI require an R&D mindset. Not all ideas will succeed, and that is fine. Learn from failures and adjust your direction.

6. **Foster collaboration:** Break down silos between business and data teams. Encourage external partnerships to bring fresh perspectives and new capabilities.

7. **Be patient:** AI adoption takes time. It is a marathon, not a sprint. It is a long-term investment, so focus on the journey, not just the immediate results.

8. **Invest in soft skills:** Communication, storytelling, and stakeholder management are just as important as technical skills. These are often what make or break a data project.

9. **Lead by example:** Leadership must communicate a clear vision and demonstrate commitment to data and AI. Transformation happens when people, not just tools, evolve.

10. **Keep learning:** AI is a fast-moving field. Stay informed, train your teams, and be ready to adapt. The journey is long, but rewarding.

Now that you have read this book and can discuss its content with your colleagues, the next step is to take action within your company, as noted in Doug Laney's "Infonomics":

> *When considering how to put information to work for your organization, it's essential to go beyond thinking and talking about information as an asset, to actually valuing and treating it as one.*

I also hope that with this book, you understand that AI is a tool with power and also limits. It is definitely not about human or AI, but about the combination of human and AI. As noted by Beena Ammanath in "Trustworthy AI":

> *Therein is the realization that AI requires human participation and judgment".*

We also need to ask ourselves where we want to go with AI, which is a more societal and philosophical question. In the end, keep in mind that the journey will take time. As noted in "Power and Prediction":

> *AI has the transformation potential of electricity, but if history is a guide, that transformation is going to be a long and bumpy ride.*

On my side, I am optimistic about data and AI. I like the vision highlighted in "Superagency": "*What could possibly go right*" with AI? Now the ball is on your side; it is up to you to create impact with data and AI. Enjoy *your* data and AI journey!

Continuous learning

I suggest three tips to continue learning in the fields of data and AI, in case you want to get more hands-on and concretely leverage data.

1. Get exposed to the data in your company. Collect data related to your job and try to gain insights using visualization and statistics to start with.

2. Try a no-code tool for machine learning (or the Python or R programming languages) and participate in a hackathon or public competition on platforms like Kaggle.

3. Read the many books mentioned throughout the book and at the end of each chapter. Try the examples proposed in the practical books.

About the Author

Dr. Sandro Saitta is a seasoned data and AI leader dedicated to helping organizations transform their analytical potential into tangible business results. As a Data & AI advisor at viadata (www.viadata.ch), he advises executives, leads corporate training programs, and supports companies in building their data capabilities, from strategy design to project execution.

Previously, he served as Head of the Industry Unit at the Swiss Data Science Center (SDSC), where he built and led a team of 20 data scientists and launched more than 25 high-impact collaborations with companies such as Richemont, Logitech, Merck, Adecco and Firmenich. Throughout his career, Sandro has worked at the intersection of business value and technical innovation. At Expedia, he led a strategic project to identify and onboard high-value hotel partners. At SICPA, he led machine learning projects to support advanced authentication technologies. At Nestlé Nespresso, he led the development of a global, data-driven forecasting system for demand planning.

Sandro holds a Ph.D. in Computer Science from EPFL. He is a strong advocate for data and AI literacy and loves connecting people. He co-founded the Swiss Association for Analytics, a nonprofit organization that promotes data science across Switzerland through events and community-building initiatives. He lectures at HEC Lausanne in the Certificate of Advanced Studies in Data Science and Management, where he helps shape the next generation of data-aware business leaders. Sandro is also a member of the executive committee of CDOIQ Europe, supporting the development of Chief Data Officers and AI leaders throughout the continent. He is also the creator of the AI Literacy Academy, a self-paced online program offering a business-focused introduction to Artificial Intelligence (www.ai-literacy-academy.com).

You can contact him at sandro.saitta@viadata.ch.

Feel free to connect on LinkedIn via the QR code below.

Glossary

AI Agents: systems that can make autonomous decisions and take actions toward defined goals, often relying on AI models for reasoning.

Algorithm: a step-by-step method used to solve a problem or perform a specific task with data.

Analytics: examining data to find patterns, trends, or insights that support business decisions.

Artificial General Intelligence (AGI): a theoretical form of AI capable of performing any intellectual task that a human can, unlike today's narrow AI.

Artificial Intelligence (AI): systems or machines that can perform tasks usually requiring human intelligence, such as learning or decision-making.

Automation: using technology to perform repetitive tasks with little or no human intervention.

Bias: an error in a model or dataset that leads to unfair or inaccurate results.

Big Data: datasets so large or complex that traditional tools cannot manage them, often described by the 3Vs: volume, variety, and velocity.

Business Problem: a specific challenge a company faces that data and AI can help to solve.

Classification: a machine learning task that assigns items to categories, such as predicting whether a customer will buy or not.

Clustering: grouping similar items together based on shared characteristics, for example used to segment customers.

Correlation: measures how two variables move in relation to each other.

CRISP-DM: Cross Industry Standard Process for Data Mining is a method for managing data projects, composed of six main steps, ranging from business understanding to deployment.

Dashboard: displays key metrics and data visualizations to monitor performance and support decisions.

Data: facts or figures collected from various sources for analysis.

Data Governance: rules and responsibilities for managing data properly within a company.

Data Mining: the process of extracting patterns, trends, or knowledge from large datasets, often considered a precursor to modern data science.

Data Quality: the degree to which data is accurate, complete, consistent, timely and reliable for its intended use.

Data Science: the process of extracting useful insights from data to better drive business decision making.

Data Scientist: A data scientist applies analytical and programming skills to extract insights from data and build predictive models.

Data Strategy: outlines how a company will manage and leverage data to achieve business goals.

Decision Tree: a machine learning algorithm that uses a tree-like structure of decisions to classify or predict outcomes.

Deep Learning: a subfield of machine learning that uses multi-layered neural networks to learn complex patterns from large amounts of data.

Deployment: the process of putting a machine learning model into use in the real world.

Forecast: a prediction based on past data, often used for sales, demand, or revenue.

Generative AI: models that create new content such as text, images, or media by learning from patterns in data.

K-Means: a popular clustering algorithm that divides data into groups based on similarity.

Label: the known output used in supervised learning, such as "buy" or "not buy."

Machine Learning (ML): allows computers to learn from data and make predictions without being explicitly programmed.

Model: in machine learning, it is a mathematical structure trained on data to make predictions or support decisions.

Natural Language Processing (NLP): a branch of AI that enables computers to understand, interpret, and generate human language.

Neural Network: a machine learning model inspired by the brain that processes information in layers.

Overfitting: happens when a model learns the training data too well but performs poorly on new data.

Pattern: a pattern (or trend) is a recurring relationship found in data.

Precision: the share of correct positive predictions among all positive predictions made.

Prediction: the result generated by a model based on input data.

Preprocessing: the steps of cleaning and preparing data before using it in a model.

Probability: a value that reflects the likelihood of an event or outcome occurring.

Recall: the share of correct positive predictions among all actual positive cases.

Regression: a technique used to predict a continuous value, like future sales.

Reinforcement Learning: teaches systems to make decisions by rewarding good actions and penalizing bad ones.

Segmentation: splitting data into distinct groups to better understand behaviors or preferences.

Statistics: a branch of mathematics focused on collecting, analyzing, and interpreting data to test hypotheses and draw conclusions.

Supervised Learning: when a model is trained with labeled data to make future predictions.

Test Set: a portion of the data used to evaluate how well a model performs.

Training Set: the data used to build and adjust the model.

Uncertainty: refers to the natural limits of predictions and the inability of a model to be perfect.

Unsupervised Learning: when models find patterns in data without predefined labels (for example clustering).

Validation: tests a model during development to tune its performance and avoid overfitting.

Visualization: helps communicate data findings through clear and effective graphics.

Index